Fooling Ourselves with Fig Leaves

Fooling Ourselves with Fig Leaves

Confusing Religiosity with Righteousness

Ed Miciano

WIPF & STOCK · Eugene, Oregon

FOOLING OURSELVES WITH FIG LEAVES
Confusing Religiosity with Righteousness

Copyright © 2016 Ed Miciano. All rights reserved. Except for brief quotations in critical publications or reviews, no part of this book may be reproduced in any manner without prior written permission from the publisher. Write: Permissions, Wipf and Stock Publishers, 199 W. 8th Ave., Suite 3, Eugene, OR 97401.

Wipf & Stock
An Imprint of Wipf and Stock Publishers
199 W. 8th Ave., Suite 3
Eugene, OR 97401

www.wipfandstock.com

PAPERBACK ISBN: 978-1-4982-3334-7
HARDCOVER ISBN: 978-1-4982-3336-1
EBOOK ISBN: 978-1-4982-3335-4

Manufactured in the U.S.A.

Unless otherwise indicated, all Scripture quotations are taken from the Holy Bible, New Living Translation, copyright © 1996, 2004, 2007, 2013, 2015 by Tyndale House Foundation. Used by permission of Tyndale House Publishers, Inc., Carol Stream, Illinois 60188. All rights reserved.

To my wife, Ana,
and our offspring,
Jonathan, Rebekah, and Jacob.

So Christ has truly set us free.
Now make sure that you stay free,
and don't get tied up again in slavery to the law.

—GAL 5:1

Contents

Acknowledgments | ix
Introduction | xi

Chapter 1   You've Got Mail | 1
Chapter 2   An Unlikely Story | 10
Chapter 3   All in Favor, Say "Aye" | 20
Chapter 4   Peter, Peter, Kosher Eater | 30
Chapter 5   Stop! In the Name of the Law | 43
Chapter 6   A Promise Is a Promise | 56
Chapter 7   Free at Last! | 67
Chapter 8   Losing My Religion | 80
Chapter 9   Two Is a Crowd | 93
Chapter 10   Take It or Leave It | 105
Chapter 11   Adding Fruit to Your Diet | 119
Chapter 12   Reap It Good | 135
Chapter 13   Just One More Thing | 149

Epilogue | 159

Acknowledgments

THIS BOOK IS THE result of a sermon series that began in 2010 and carried on until the fall of 2011. I want to thank the awesome members of Bridgepoint Community Church for journeying through the series with me. You have made ministry work a joy, and I am grateful for the opportunity to be your shepherd.

I also want to thank Mrs. Cynthia de Castro and Mrs. Grace Pangilinan for helping me prepare the manuscript for publication. I especially appreciate my colleague Dr. Abraham Ruelas for his invaluable advice and recommendations on how to improve various sections of this book. This project would simply not be possible without his expert assistance.

I am grateful for the unconditional love and patience of my precious wife, Ana. God knows all our needs, and he knew how much I needed you in my life. You are a gift like no other.

Finally, I want to acknowledge my awesome children, Jonathan, Rebekah, and Jacob. I imagine living in a pastor's household has had its share of joys and challenges. I pray, however, that your mom and I have succeeded in teaching you to love the Lord with all your hearts, your souls, your minds, and your strength.

Introduction

> Then the eyes of both of them were opened,
> and they realized they were naked;
> so they sewed fig leaves together
> and made coverings for themselves.
>
> —GEN 3:7

THE STORY IS AN all too familiar one. Adam and Eve had just disobeyed a divine directive that severed their relationship with God. In an attempt to cover up their sin and be made right in the eyes of the Lord, they fashioned together some fig leaves and covered their nakedness. What appears to merely be poor fashion judgment actually proves to be one of the most epic failures in Bible history.

If by "religion" we mean the attempt to make oneself right with God through self-effort, then I believe the world's first religion was the fig leaf. Fig leaves represent an attempt at righteousness that proves to be an inadequate covering for human sinfulness. We know this because God himself rejected Adam and Eve's cover-up. You see, Adam and Eve were simply fooling themselves with fig leaves, because the leaves they used had no ability to hide their wickedness from God, nor could they restore the relationship with God marred by sin.

People today continue to fool themselves with fig leaves. We fool ourselves when we think that belonging to the right religion saves us from sin, or that performing religious acts have salvific merit, and when we trust in our religious fervor more than we trust in God. Fig leaves are deceptive because they give a false notion of covering without truly granting anyone right standing with God. It is confusing religiosity with righteousness.

In the first century, Paul had to confront the problem of religious deception among believers in a city called Galatia. False teachers had infiltrated the church and were introducing a new kind of fig leaf in the form of bondage to religious law. The apostle addressed this matter by writing a letter to the church. The result is what we now know as the Epistle to the Galatians, an ancient document that is forever preserved in the pages of Holy Scripture.

In *Fooling Ourselves with Fig Leaves*, we will examine the content and message of this letter with the hope of understanding how to guard ourselves from religious deception and discover the gift of true righteousness through faith in Jesus Christ.

1

You've Got Mail

Galatians 1:1–5

I MUST CONFESS, I can't remember the last time I sat down with a pen in hand and took my time to write a thoughtful letter. Sadly, the art of letter writing seems to be a lost skill in this modern age of electronic mail and mobile texting. I imagine that postal workers wake up each day concerned about how long it will be before their industry will be largely unnecessary (God forbid!). Needless to say, all this has changed the landscape of communication and human connectedness.

Conversely, the ancient world was very much marked by, if not dependent on, letter writing as an important means of communication. It was at the heart of how people dialogued when face-to-face conversations were not possible. In fact, the Roman Empire took this form of communication so seriously that it developed the most advanced postal system of its day. We are not certain whether the early church and its leaders made extensive use of this system, but it is conceivable that they would have. The Apostle Paul, for instance, would have benefited much from this service, considering he wrote quite a number of letters in his lifetime.

Paul is credited with writing almost half of the books that make up the New Testament. All of his books came in the form of epistles, or letters. Although I am certain Paul would rather have conveyed his messages in person, the fact that he could not be in several places at once made writing letters the next best option to communicate his thoughts and instructions to the churches. Letters, therefore, became one of the principle tools for spreading the gospel message in the first century.

Paul wrote many such letters in the course of his ministry. Some were written to individuals, while others were written to churches. The epistle to the Galatians is an example of the latter. It is also believed to be the first (or one of the first) among many that Paul wrote. This makes it a valuable resource for understanding Paul's own development as an apostle and a leading theologian of the ancient church.

Every letter is written for a specific purpose with a particular audience in mind. In order to appreciate and understand the message of Galatians, it is important to take time to know who wrote this letter, to whom it was written, and what prompted its composition.

The Author: Paul the Apostle

In this letter, Paul identifies himself as its author. This in itself is not unusual. What is unusual, however, is the manner in which he described himself. In Gal 1:1, he wrote, "This is a letter from Paul, an apostle. I was not appointed by any group of people or any human authority, but by Jesus Christ himself and by God the Father, who raised Jesus from the dead." Immediately, one senses an authoritative tone to Paul's introduction. It is almost as if he wanted to establish his apostolic credentials from the very onset of his letter. The reason for this becomes obvious once we understand the circumstances that brought about this epistle.

The Galatian churches had been plagued with false teachers who sought to destroy what Paul had accomplished among the churches in the region. The primary method employed by these false teachers was to question the authenticity of Paul's apostleship. They managed to convince some of the Galatians to reject Paul because he was not an original eyewitness to the earthly ministry of Christ and did not receive his apostolic calling prior to the death and resurrection of Jesus. It was believed by some that these were the two important criteria for true apostleship. If so, then the term "apostle" can only be used to refer to the twelve original followers of Jesus. However, there is nothing in Scripture that insists on such a limited understanding of what an apostle is, and, as such, the scope of apostleship supersedes the circle of the original twelve.

By definition, the word "apostle," from the Greek *apostolos*, simply means "one who is sent with a message." While it is true that the original twelve followers of Christ fit this definition, there were also others who fit this description. Take, for instance, other eyewitnesses to the resurrection of Jesus. In 1 Cor 15, shortly after asserting that Peter and the (original) apostles saw the resurrected Christ, Paul goes on to identify the other witnesses as "James and . . . all the apostles" (1 Cor 15:7). The James mentioned here is not one of the original twelve but rather the brother of the Lord Jesus, the eventual head of the Jerusalem church. Likewise, the apostles mentioned in verse seven refer to those who became apostles after the ministry of the twelve was well established. Furthermore, in 1 Thess 2:7, Paul referred to himself, along with Silas and Timothy, as apostles when he wrote, "As apostles of Christ, we certainly had a right to make some demands of you."

So in what sense is Paul an apostle? Although he was not necessarily an eyewitness to the earthly ministry of Jesus, Paul "saw" the Lord during his Damascus road conversion. Also, it was then that the Lord commissioned Paul to be a messenger of the gospel. In fact, the Lord affirmed this call to another believer named Ananias when he said, "For Saul is my chosen instrument to take my message to the Gentiles and to kings, as well as to the people of Israel" (Acts 9:15). In this sense, Paul is an authentic apostle even though he became one, in his words, "at a wrong time" (1 Cor 15:8), meaning that he was saved and called *after* the resurrection rather than beforehand. Paul is therefore right to claim that his apostleship was established directly by Christ without any human agency. This is, in essence, the highest form of apostolic authentication.

Paul's reference to God as the "one who raised Jesus from the dead" is an important assertion that will give credence to his subsequent argument regarding the sufficiency of Christ's redemptive work. The power of God to raise the dead is the same power that liberates believers from the clutches of sin and releases us to enjoy the freedom we have in Christ. The life of Paul serves as a perfect example of this important salvific principle.

The Recipient: The Churches of Galatia

Regarding his intended audience, Paul wrote, "All the brothers and sisters here join me in sending this letter to the churches of Galatia" (Gal 1:2). Although we know this letter was written to a group of churches as opposed to one particular local church, the exact location of Galatia is not as easy to identify as it might seem. Also, our ability to determine when this letter was written is contingent upon knowing who these Galatians believers were.

There are currently two schools of thought regarding what Paul meant by the churches in Galatia. The term "Galatian" can have an ethnic meaning or a political meaning. Ethnically, it refers to the group of people the French call the Gauls. They occupied the region known as Northern Galatia. There is little evidence that Paul ever visited this northern region of Galatia.

Politically, "Galatian" refers to the people who live in the region known as Southern Galatia, an area conquered by the Romans in 189 BC. This southern region was actually included in the list of places Paul visited during his first missionary journey. Because of this and other circumstantial considerations, many scholars today believe the Galatian epistle was addressed to those in the south. If this is the case, Paul most likely wrote this letter in AD 49 while he was in Corinth, just prior to the First Jerusalem Council in AD 50. This position, although popular, is not fully conclusive.

Although we may never fully ascertain whether Paul was writing to the Galatians in the north or the south, his opening words to them are nonetheless meaningful. He wrote, "May God our Father and the Lord Jesus Christ give you grace and peace. Jesus gave his life for our sins, just as God our Father planned, in order to rescue us from this evil world in which we live. All glory to God forever and ever! Amen" (Gal 1:3–5).

The greeting of "grace and peace" was common in the first century, but it has special meaning in this letter. The word "grace" conveys the idea of God's bestowed favor. Theologically, it is especially significant because it includes the notion that such favor is neither merited nor deserved by its recipients. We have done nothing to earn God's forgiveness. The blessings of righteousness and eternal life are "gifts" in the purest sense of the word. God gives them to us with no consideration of our ability to obtain them on our own. The only condition placed on us is that we wholeheartedly receive this gift and cherish it as the priceless treasure that it is.

"Peace," on the other hand, describes the result of living in the state of grace. Whereas peace is commonly understood as the absence of turmoil, the biblical concept of peace carries a somewhat nuanced meaning. Peace is not so much the absence of trouble as it is the presence of God in the midst of turmoil. This peace that surpasses human understanding can only come from God himself. Because we are saved by his grace through faith, we become able to live in peace even though the rest of our earthly existence may be riddled with external strife and conflict.

Paul alluded to the sacrificial death of Christ—the laying down of his life on the cross—as God's way of dealing with the problem of sin and human depravity. We are rescued from the consequences of sin and are lifted from our fallen state only because of the redemptive work of Jesus Christ. This means that no one is able to point to religiosity as the source of one's righteousness because a right standing with God is, as we have argued, a gift. The benefit of this gift is that we are rescued from this evil world. That is not to say that we immediately cease living in an evil world but rather that we no longer live under the influence and subsequent consequence of sin.

This is the true freedom of the human soul. And because of the conditions under which we obtain this freedom, it is fitting to glorify God forever and ever, because there is no other way, and there never will be another way for us to be free. Jesus himself said, "So if the Son sets you free, you are truly free" (John 8:35).

The Reason: To Expose the Lie of False Teachers

When I first came to the United States, virtually no one communicated through email or cell phones. I was about nine thousand miles from home, and the only cost-effective way to connect with my family and friends was through letters delivered by the postal service. It would literally take weeks, if not months, between sending and receiving letters. Each day after class, I would rush home to stick my hand in the mailbox, hoping there would be a letter for me. Oh, how I looked forward to reading anything and everything that came from the Philippines. They could never replace face-to-face conversations, but they were better than nothing.

Now before I over-romanticize the notion of receiving mail, there are times when a letter arrives that you wish had never come, such as a bill from the IRS or a note informing you of the death of a loved one. Some letters are just difficult to read. I'm fairly sure this is how the Galatians felt about reading Paul's letter. After all, this was not a lighthearted correspondence from an acquaintance; rather, it was a stern letter of rebuke and correction from a concerned spiritual father.

Normally, Paul began his letters with words of praise and thanksgiving for the individual or church he was addressing. For instance, in his letter to the Philippians Paul wrote, "Every time I think of you, I give thanks to my God" (Phil 1:3). However, such accolades are noticeably absent in the letter to the Galatians. Instead, the apostle begins by saying, "I am shocked that you are turning away from God, who called you to himself through the loving mercy of Christ. You are following a different way that pretends to be the good news" (Gal 1:6). Not one to offer the Galatians insincere flattery, Paul gets straight to the point. It is easy to imagine him with a grim look on his face as he wrote (or dictated) this line. In ancient literature, this manner of conveying anger and angst is found only in the harshest of situations. In Paul's mind, the Galatian controversy was so grave that it merited this kind of approach.

The Galatian epistle is often classified as deliberative rhetoric. This refers to an ancient form of argumentation in which the speaker presents a case with the intention of convincing the listener to change a particular perspective and, consequently, a behavior. Paul employs this writing style throughout the rest of the letter. He does so with deliberately chosen words that convey the rationale for his argument as well as the emotions he feels while he writes.

Paul is in shock. He knew these people well. Because of his ministry, the Galatians were fully exposed to the truth of the gospel. They were previously living as pagans but were soon blessed to be drawn to God and his mercy. As a result, they heard the gospel, the good news, and were saved by grace through faith. But now they were entertaining false teachers who persuaded them to adhere to a *different way*. They received a message that pretended to be the gospel but instead was a deceptive message that ran contrary to the one Paul had preached.

In effect, the Galatians were guilty of desertion, for they had turned away from the truth of God and exchanged it for a lie. The term "turning away" is based on the imagery of a military revolt—a mutiny in which allegiance shifts from one party to another. If, as Paul asserts, the Galatians were once called to God, they were now walking away from God. They were not just deserting an ideology, they were deserting a person—one who loved them and showered them with the gifts of mercy, forgiveness, and salvation. This was no small offense.

Although the false teachers are not mentioned by name, their actions are described as manipulative trickery. Speaking of their message and method, Paul said, "but his is not the good news at all. You are being fooled by those who deliberately twist the truth concerning" Christ (Gal 1:7). These false teachers were not sincere people who happened to be wrong. They were troublemakers who were deliberately misleading the Galatians by distorting the message Paul had originally brought to these churches. So on the one hand, the false teachers were guilty of maliciously misleading the Galatians to follow a different gospel. The Galatians, on the other hand, demonstrated a lack of maturity and discernment in that they were easily conned into accepting this lie.

What do we know about the false teachers and their message? Scholars have suggested that they were early Judaizers who insisted that becoming a Christian required adherence to Jewish law. The first group of Christians recorded in Scripture happen to be people who were culturally Jewish. As such, they had an active Jewish lifestyle that coincided with their newfound faith in Jesus Christ. They practiced circumcision, were involved in regular temple worship, and continued to observe the food laws stipulated in the Torah.

The problem arose when the Christian gospel started to spread among Gentiles. Suddenly, there were people who were putting their faith in Christ in spite of the fact that they had no background in Jewish religiosity. The church, therefore, had to take a position on this matter. The issue at hand was simple: Should Gentile converts be subject to Jewish law? This question was debated at the First Council of Jerusalem (Acts 15). In the end, the church agreed that Gentiles who became Christians did not have to adhere to most of the Jewish laws, since the only requirement for salvation was faith in the Lord Jesus Christ. The Judaizers, however, did not agree with this position and continued to insist that Gentile converts had to observe all the laws given to the Jewish people. Hence, this "other gospel" that was being preached to the Galatians.

Misleading people with a false message was such a serious matter that Paul pronounced a judgment on anyone trying to do so. He told the Galatians,

> Let God's curse fall on anyone, including us or even an angel from heaven, who preaches a different kind of good news than the one we preached to you. I say again what we have said before: If anyone preaches any other good news than the one you welcomed, let that person be cursed. (Gal 1:8–9)

The modern reader might not immediately notice how forceful this statement is. Perhaps because the concept of being *cursed* is often understood as childish pronouncements of anger. But consider how the original reader would have understood this warning from Paul. The idea of a curse, from the term *anathemas*, has to do with the damnation of the soul. A cursed soul is cast out of the realm of God's redemption and results in eternal separation from God. This is just about the strongest term Paul could have used as a warning. After all, who in their right mind would want to suffer this fate?

The scope of this warning is equally fascinating. No one is off the hook from the danger of this curse. Paul stressed that neither he nor angelic messengers are exceptions to this rule. This is especially appropriate because it was common for first-century mystics to claim angels as the source of their revelation. Of course, two thousand years later, not much has changed. I am reminded of the praise given to the believers in Berea. As Luke recounts,

> And the people of Berea were more open-minded than those in Thessalonica, and they listened eagerly to Paul's message. They searched the Scriptures day after day to check up on Paul and Silas, to see if they were really teaching the truth. (Acts 17:11)

Like the Bereans, every believer must be personally responsible for protecting his or her mind and heart from deceit. When you open yourself to a false gospel, you cannot get away with saying, "But I trusted this person and so I believed what he said." Everyone is subject to careful examination. This is not a threat to those who speak the truth, because such a person is never afraid of being scrutinized.

The true messengers of God understand that there are many angles at which a pole can be slanted but only one angle at which it stands perfectly erect. The gospel of Jesus Christ is a firmly planted pole amidst countless slanted ones. Any message that does not square with the gospel is to be rejected, and its messengers are to be cursed. So emphatic is Paul about this that he even repeats the same warning in verse nine. He is not merely being hypothetical because, as he reminds the Galatians, they already welcomed a false gospel, and therefore the false teachers were already under a curse.

Paul ends this section of the letter with a word of clarification aimed at those who questioned his integrity. He said, "Obviously, I'm not trying to win the approval of people, but of God. If pleasing people were my goal, I would not be Christ's servant" (Gal 1:10). Pleasing God rather than men was a common theme among philosophers in the first century. As a rule, a person who seeks to please people at the expense of telling the truth is not to be trusted. It is little wonder that politicians are among the least trusted people in the world.

Paul was no politician. He was not a people-pleaser; he was a God-pleaser. With the opening words of this letter, Paul showed he was willing to speak the truth whether or not it was the popular thing to say. He was not as interested in the Galatians' happiness as much as he was interested in their holiness. Like Paul, a true and humble servant of Christ cannot live for the approval of people. We cannot serve, and therefore please, two masters. Christ demands full allegiance from us—nothing more, nothing less.

It is amazing how a letter written two thousand years ago can be so relevant to us today. As in the days of the Galatians, these times are marked by false messengers who are screaming out lies in the hope that we will buy into their counterfeit message. They are slick communicators who can even come across as angels of light. But don't be fooled. These false teachers are living under a curse that will be shared by those who fail to uphold God's truth and instead welcome another gospel, which is really no gospel at all.

2

An Unlikely Story

Galatians 1:11–24

SUSPICIOUS. YOU WOULD BE if you heard that a staunch critic suddenly turned into an advocate for a cause once vilified. Imagine if Rush Limbaugh endorsed a democrat, or if the late Colonel Sanders became a vegetarian, or even if an anti-war activist enlisted in the army. Such head-scratchers are virtually unthinkable, but, as the saying goes, truth is often stranger than fiction. Take the case of Paul.

In the opening lines of his epistle to the Galatians, the Apostle Paul reprimanded the Galatian churches for aligning themselves with zealots who were all too eager to distort the gospel in the name of religion. Yet wasn't Paul himself once guilty of this very offense? Was this the same Paul that oversaw the persecution of the Christian church in the name of his religion? The answer, of course, is yes. But instead of viewing this as a problem, Paul actually presents this as a reasonably convincing argument for his case. That he, one of the most unlikely candidates for apostleship, actually became a spokesperson for the gospel is an incredible testimony of the power of God to transform a life and redeem it for his glory.

The suspicious reader might have asked, "What qualifies Paul to speak to us with such authority, and how do we know his gospel is true?" After all, didn't Paul himself just say that even he should be subject to scrutiny when discerning the validity of a heavenly message? In response to this, Paul offers his personal story to undergird his rationale for being so forceful in dealing with his Galatian readers. There are four elements that make up this unlikely, yet fascinating story.

Paul's Source of Revelation

Ancient letters often included a narrative section that served a specific purpose. In this case, Paul wanted to demonstrate the integrity of his character in light of all the accusations launched against him by the false teachers. In his mind, failure to clear his reputation would weaken the strength of his discourse, because the integrity of the messenger and the content of the message must be consistent. Just as you would not take health advice from an overweight slob, the Galatians were not about to take spiritual advice from Paul if they were not confident he was spiritually fit to speak to this issue. By upholding his integrity as an apostle, Paul puts himself in a position to speak authoritatively to the Galatian believers.

The narrative portion of this letter comes in the form of a brief autobiography. Paul first introduces the story of his conversion by saying,

> Dear brothers and sisters, I want you to understand that the gospel message I preach is not based on mere human reasoning. I received my message from no human source, and no one taught me. Instead, I received it by direct revelation from Jesus Christ. (Gal 1:11–12)

Paul clarifies his thesis from the onset. By saying, "I want you to understand," he appeals to readers' ability to judge the veracity of his claims. And since it is in direct contraction to his opponents' claims, to trust Paul means that the Galatians should logically refuse to trust the false teachers. And why is Paul's teaching more trustworthy? Primarily because it has a divine source and origin.

The message Paul is preaching did not come as the result of his genius, nor was he instructed by any other person; his source was simply not human but divine. For Paul, human logic was not a sufficient basis for authenticating the Christian gospel. The ability to intellectualize God's Word, albeit impressive, still falls short of proving that it is indeed from God. In fact, God has a history of using the simpleminded to convey his message to the world so effectively that one cannot credit the person for its potency but must instead give all the credit and glory to God alone. In another letter, Paul said God's power "works best in weakness" (2 Cor 12:9).

In identifying the source of his gospel, Paul appeals to direct revelation—that is, God revealed the good news to him without channeling it through any human agency. Remarkably, Paul is not timid about making such an audacious claim. He is, in essence, claiming the same source of authority as that of the original apostles. Paul is a firsthand recipient of God's message, and this qualifies him to testify with the authority of a judicial witness as well as an ambassador.

A closer look at the gospel message will show that what Paul claims actually makes sense. You see, the gospel story is completely counterintuitive to human sensibility. Human argumentation, in order to be convincing, depends on a series of strong ideas building on even stronger ideas. So in this sense, who in their right mind would create a gospel based on a crucifixion and resurrection claim?

Crucifixion, a form of Roman capital punishment, was not viewed as a stepping-stone to power but rather a symbol of defeat. It represented the fate of despicable criminals who deserved to be wiped off the face of the earth. Yet the gospel contends that our salvation is grounded on the crucifixion of a man. This notion would have been simply too ridiculous to entertain had it not actually effected the transformation of lives and the growth of the church.

As if that was not unusual enough, those who put their trust in the redemptive power of Christ's crucifixion are also told to believe that this same Jesus rose from the dead three days later! This not only sounds ridiculous, it is seemingly unnecessary. Why would anyone subject their movement to concepts that are so difficult to explain or even substantiate? Wouldn't it have been easier to just say that Jesus taught nice things and that if you follow a bunch of religious stipulations, you will be a righteous person? Yet precisely because the gospel claim is so audacious, the Galatian reader is left to make one of two conclusions: Paul is either hopelessly deluded, or he is telling the truth. And for Paul, what better way to show he is telling the truth than by demonstrating the transformative power of the gospel in his own life?

Paul's Past

Paul had a reputation, but it wasn't necessarily a good one. He told the Galatians, "You know what I was like when I followed the Jewish religion—how I violently persecuted God's church. I did my best to destroy it. I was far ahead of my fellow Jews in my zeal for the traditions of my ancestors" (Gal 1:13–14).

Every movement has its zealots. In first-century Judaism, his name was Saul (he eventually changed it to Paul after he became an apostle of Christ). He had extensive training in Jewish law and had lived the strict lifestyle of a Pharisee. Even today, the term "Pharisee" conjures images of a religious fanatic of the highest degree. As with all Pharisees, Saul strictly observed the Jewish law and was committed to a number of religious duties such as temple worship, fasting and prayer, and ritual cleansing. The goal of the Pharisees was to incorporate Jewish law into everyday life. As such, they tended to be legalistic in their approach to spirituality. Furthermore, it was not uncommon for Pharisees to be judgmental toward those who did not share their zeal for the faith.

Saul was not only religious, he was militantly religious. He reminded the Galatians of how he "violently persecuted God's church." A perfect example of this would be the martyrdom of Stephen. According to Luke,

> The Jewish leaders were infuriated by Stephen's accusation, and they shook their fists at him in rage. But Stephen, full of the Holy Spirit, gazed steadily into heaven and saw the glory of God, and he saw Jesus standing in the place of honor at God's right hand. And he told them, "Look, I see the heavens opened and the Son of Man standing in the place of honor at God's right hand!" They put their hands over their ears and began shouting. The rushed at him and dragged him out of the city and began to stone him. His accusers took off their coats and laid them at the feet of a young man named Saul. As they stoned him, Stephen prayed, "Lord Jesus, receive my spirit." He fell to his knees, shouting, "Lord, don't charge them with this sin!" And with that, he died. (Acts 7:54–60)

Although Luke does not say whether Saul, described here as a young man, actually participated in Stephen's stoning, it is clear that he fully sanctioned the killing, for Luke continued on to say, "Saul was one of the witnesses, and he agreed completely with the killing of Stephen" (Acts 8:1). Following Stephen's death, Saul continued to wreak havoc among Christian believers, going everywhere he could to destroy churches and imprison Christ's followers. Soon after, he headed off to Damascus to continue his witch hunt and persecute more disciples of Jesus Christ.

Saul's credentials as a Jewish zealot are described further in another of his letters. Writing to the believers in Philippi, he said,

> I was circumcised when I was eight days old. I am a pure-blooded citizen of Israel and a member of the tribe of Benjamin—a real Hebrew if there ever was one! I was a member of the Pharisees, who demand the strictest obedience to the Jewish law. I was so zealous that I harshly persecuted the church. And as for righteousness, I obeyed the law without fault. (Phil 3:4–6)

Clearly no one, not even the false teachers in Galatia, could claim to have been more fanatical about Judaism than Saul was. He superseded his rivals in almost every aspect of the law. To top it off, Saul was a prince among the persecutors of Christians. There was simply no way to brush Paul off as an ignoramus who had no authority to confront false teachers. The Galatians had to fully acknowledge that.

I appreciate how honest Paul was about his past. He could have covered up this part of the story and instead beefed up his credentials as a great apostle. But to do so would be to deny the role of grace in his conversion.

Paul did not speak of his former zeal with pride, for as an apostle of Christ, how could he be proud of harming Christ's followers? However, acknowledgement of his dark past creates an incredible backdrop for explaining how powerful the gospel is. If the power of Christ's good news is capable of redeeming one as lost as he, then surely no one lives outside the realm of God's saving grace.

Paul's Turning Point

How did one of the strongest critics of the early church movement suddenly become one of its greatest advocates? Paul gives all the credit to God. He said to the Galatians, "But even before I was born, God chose me and called me by his marvelous grace. Then it pleased him to reveal his Son to me so that I would proclaim the good news about Jesus to the Gentiles" (Gal 1:15–16a). His words parallel that of the great prophet Jeremiah, who declared, "I knew you before I formed you in your mother's womb. Before you were born I set you apart and appointed you as my prophet to the nations" (Jer 1:5).

The calling of Paul is recorded with full drama. Luke documented this event:

> As he was approaching Damascus on this mission, a light from heaven suddenly shone down around him. He fell to the ground and heard a voice saying to him, "Saul! Saul! Why are you persecuting me? "Who are you, lord?" Saul asked. And the voice replied, "I am Jesus, the one you are persecuting! Now get up and go into the city, and you will be told what you must do." (Acts 9:3–6)

Paul identifies two acts of God that resulted in his dramatic turnaround. First, God chose him and called him by grace. Here Paul brings up the doctrine of election and links it to his own experience. By "election," we simply refer to God's choice to bestow the blessing of salvation upon an individual. Jesus himself reminded us, "You didn't choose me . . . I chose you . . . I appointed you to go and produce lasting fruit" (John 15:16).

The adage "even before I was born" emphasizes the gracious nature of election. If God chooses us before we are born, then obviously there is nothing we had done to earn salvation—it was truly a gift of God. This understanding of election tends to trouble some people because they feel it robs us of our ability to exercise free will. But how free is our will when we are so corrupted by our sinful nature? Take, for instance, a bird with broken wings. Even if it willed itself to fly, it has no power to exercise that will. Likewise, Paul would argue that our spiritual brokenness keeps us from doing anything to save ourselves, no matter how strong we will it to be. We are utterly at the mercy of a loving God who calls us to himself by his marvelous grace.

Secondly, God revealed Christ to Paul so that Paul would be enabled to preach the gospel. It gives God pleasure to invite us to partner with him in his mission. I sometimes wonder why he does this. Wouldn't the job be done more perfectly if we humans did not get involved? Indeed, God has no need for us, but in his love he blesses us with the privilege of being a part of the great task of harvesting the souls of lost men and women. And specifically for Paul, God wanted him to proclaim the gospel to the Gentile world.

At this point, Paul once again addresses those who question the legitimacy of his apostleship by clarifying that human intervention was not a factor in his call to be an apostle of the Lord Jesus Christ. He writes,

> When this happened, I did not rush out to consult with any human being. Nor did I go up to Jerusalem to consult with those who were apostles before I was. Instead, I went away into Arabia, and later I returned to the city of Damascus. Then three years later I went to Jerusalem to get to know Peter, and I stayed with him for fifteen days. The only other apostle I met at that time was James, the Lord's brother. I declare before God that what I am writing to you is not a lie. After that visit I went north into the provinces of Syria and Cilicia. (Gal 1:16b-21)

Even after his encounter with Christ, Paul did not seek out human intervention to validate his conversion experience. Instead of going to Jerusalem (a logical choice, since that is where the apostolic church was headquartered), he went to Arabia. By distancing himself from Peter and the other Jerusalem leaders, Paul was showing the Galatians readers that he was not a subordinate of the original apostles; rather, he was their equal because his apostolic call came from the same Lord Jesus Christ.

By "Arabia," Paul was likely referring to Nabataea, the area around the city of Damascus in Syria. In terms of a timeline, this trip could be inserted between Acts 9:22 (when he was in Damascus preaching the gospel) and Acts 9:23 (when friends had to secretly whisk him away from the city because of a threat on his life). What exactly he did in Arabia is uncertain, but it is conceivable that Paul would have used this time for contemplation and study. Anyone who had undergone a conversion as dramatic as Paul's would certainly have needed to debrief as well as to prepare for the intimidating task of bringing the gospel message to the Gentile world.

Paul eventually did go to Jerusalem, but it was not to seek human approval for his calling. Three years after his stay in Damascus, he met Peter in Jerusalem. We are not told what transpired during that visit. Perhaps Paul purposely withheld such information in order to clarify that the nature of his visit was personal, not official. Undoubtedly, Peter and Paul would have exchanged stories about their encounters with Christ and how privileged they each were for being counted worthy to proclaim such a marvelous gospel. All we know is that Paul's visit was brief, roughly two weeks long.

Furthermore, Paul also took time to visit the Apostle James. There are a number of men in the New Testament who have this name. Upon a first reading, one might tend to think of James, brother of John, both of whom were among the original twelve apostles of Christ. But we know that this was not the James he met because Paul was kind enough to identify this one as "the Lord's brother."

Christendom is divided on the question of whether or not Jesus was an only child. There are those who hold to the dogma known as the "Perpetual Virginity of Mary." This theory suggests that since Mary was forever a virgin, she had no other children after the miraculous birth of Jesus. Those who hold to this belief do so for largely noble reasons. Unfortunately, there is nothing in Scripture to substantiate this claim. On the contrary, there are a number of biblical references to support the notion that Joseph and Mary went on to have other children after Jesus was born. No one in the first century would have thought it unusual for a legitimately married couple to have several children. In fact, in that culture, it was virtually expected that couples such as Joseph and Mary would have more than one child.

An Unlikely Story

A couple of things should be considered regarding this issue. First of all, the Bible says that Joseph and Mary did not have marital relations until after Jesus was born (Matt 1:25). Second, although Jesus is called the "only" Son of the Father (God), he is called Mary's "firstborn" (Luke 2:7). Third, Mary's other children are mentioned by name in Matt 13:55-56, which reads, "Isn't this the carpenter's son? Isn't his mother's name Mary, and aren't his brothers James, Joseph, Simon and Judas? Aren't all his sisters with us? Where then did this man get all these things?" Mark 6:1-6 and Luke 4:16-30 also make similar references. As we can see from these passages, Jesus had four brothers and at least two sisters, and one of the brothers mentioned by name was James.

James did not appear to be a follower of Christ prior to the crucifixion and resurrection. Think about it, would *you* have believed your own brother if he claimed to be the Messiah? I know I wouldn't (you'd know what I mean if you knew my brothers). There was even a time when the brothers taunted Jesus to perform miracles, as if to mock his claim of being the Messiah. According to John,

> But soon it was time for the Jewish Festival of Shelters, and Jesus' brother said to him, "Leave here and go to Judea, where your followers can see your miracles! You can't become famous if you hide like this! If you can do such wonderful things, show yourself to the world!" For even his brothers didn't believe in him. (John 7:2-5)

James may not have been an early Christian believer, but the resurrection may have been enough to convince him that Jesus was who he said he was. Subsequently, he became a believer. Not only that, he also became an apostle and was appointed leader of the church in Jerusalem. The next time you are frustrated that your family members don't accept your faith, remember that even Jesus took a while to convince his own brothers.

After mentioning his brief encounter with James, Paul said, "I declare before God that what I am writing to you is not a lie." Such a phrase was often used as an oath to establish one's integrity in a court of law. In the modern world, we make similar statements, but for the most part we take such oaths lightly. When we say things like, "Cross my heart," or "I swear," we are usually making affirmations that are not legally binding. But in the ancient world, oaths were taken very seriously. It was believed that if a person violated an oath, God himself would personally punish that individual. For that reason, a person's oath was almost always received as a guarantee that their testimony could be trusted. In this case, Paul probably made an oath in direct response to accusations that he was not speaking the truth to the Galatians when he first ministered among them.

Paul ends this portion of his conversion story by stating that after visiting Jerusalem, he traveled north and ministered in the provinces of Syria and Cilicia. The mention of these visits (recorded in Acts 9, 11, and 13) is significant because Paul wants the Galatians to know that not only was he free from the jurisdiction of the other apostles, he actually had his own apostolic jurisdiction over regions not covered by the original apostles.

Paul's Testimony

Because Paul initially stayed away from the usual centers of apostolic activity, he did not have the chance to build personal relationships with the Christians in those areas. It would actually be several more years before Paul became a household name among the churches in the region surrounding Jerusalem and Judea. Yet in spite of this, the story of his conversion seems to have been widespread. He told the Galatians,

> And still the Christians in the churches in Judea didn't know me personally. All they knew was that the people were saying, "The one who used to persecute us is now preaching the very faith he tried to destroy!" And they praised God because of me. (Gal 1:22–24)

What a testimony! Paul's reputation had indeed preceded him. Prior to his conversion, it was quite well known that he was a staunch enemy of the church and an aggressive persecutor of Christians. Thankfully, after his conversion, it became equally well known that Paul was now a follower of Christ, and what's more, he was also a preacher of the gospel. Both in the ancient world and in modern times, it is acknowledged that the conversion of a persecutor served as one of the strongest evidence of God's power to change anyone. For this reason, Paul confidently declared to the Roman church,

> For I am not ashamed of this good news about Christ. It is the power of God at work, saving everyone who believes—Jews first and also Gentiles. This good news tells us how God makes us right in his sight. This is accomplished from start to finish by faith. As the Scriptures say, "It is through faith that a righteous person has life. (Rom 1:16–17)

This means that the same power that transformed Paul is able to transform you and me today.

The result of Paul's conversion testimony was simple—the people gave praise to God because of him. As with all miracles, such unlikely conversions ought to lead others to glorify God. Conversely, this serves as a warning to those who would use the name of Christ and the gospel to gain the praise of people.

If we are saved by the grace, mercy, and power of Christ, then you and I have a story to tell. Like Paul, let us not be ashamed to make it known how God took wretches like us and turned us into his friends and ambassadors. Every conversion story is an unlikely story, but don't be fooled—the love of God is able to accomplish even that which we find difficult to imagine. To him be all the glory!

3

All in Favor, Say "Aye"
Galatians 2:1–10

IN 1992, THE ACQUITTAL of four police officers accused of the beating of Rodney King sparked a massive riot in Los Angeles. At the height of the resulting mayhem, King himself appeared on television to appeal for peace and order. It was then that he uttered the now famous question, "Can we all get along?"

Getting along with others has been idealized ever since humanity has been at odds with itself. In beauty pageants, at least one contestant is bound to address the issue of world peace. Placards at anti-war rallies are dominated with slogans such as "Give peace a chance" and "War is not the answer." In his famous anthem, *Imagine*, John Lennon challenged us to dream up a world relieved of national boundaries, religious factions, and competing ideologies.

Surely there is nothing wrong with the desire to live in a peaceful world. I know I dream of it almost every day. But meanwhile, back on planet earth, we are forced to contend with the reality of conflict. In spite of even the most sincere effort to get along, there are times when we are simply unable to reach an agreement with others on certain issues. For better or worse, the church has not been spared from this reality.

In the first century, it did not take long after the death and resurrection of Christ for divisive issues to plague the early church. Foremost among these was the matter of how to deal with Gentile converts. Specifically, it centered on the question of whether or not Gentile believers should be circumcised (under Jewish customs) and be subject to Jewish law. In the second chapter of his letter to the Galatians, Paul addressed this subject by first clarifying that he and the Jerusalem apostles were in full agreement on the position taken by the church and that failure to align themselves with him puts the Galatians in the same camp as the false teachers.

One major challenge Paul had in making his case was the accusation that he was making a big deal out of nothing. But was the Galatian controversy really just a minor nuisance? Could it be that the issue at hand was indeed a major threat to the existence of the early church? Sometimes it isn't easy to determine which is which. Paul, however, was not going to take the chance of treating this too casually only to risk it becoming an issue that could later destroy the missionary endeavors of the Christian church. He had to nip this bud while it was young and not give it a chance to mature any further.

Paul's Gospel Challenged

Three years after his conversion, Paul went to Jerusalem for a brief visit. He did not remain there because his apostolic call was to bring the gospel to Gentiles, not Jews. However, many years later, a crisis made it necessary for Paul to return. He wrote,

> Then fourteen years later I went back to Jerusalem again, this time with Barnabas; and Titus came along, too. I went there because God revealed to me that I should go. While I was there I met privately with those considered to be leaders of the church and shared with them the message I had been preaching to the Gentiles. I wanted to make sure that we were in agreement, for fear that all my efforts had been wasted and I was running the race for nothing. (Gal 2:1–2)

There is a deep sense of urgency when Paul declares that "God revealed to me that I should go." This is not to suggest that none of the Jerusalem apostles extended an invitation for him to come, but regardless of human agency, Paul was now in Jerusalem because it was ultimately a divine appointment.

Many scholars believe that this event coincides with the First Council of Jerusalem, which is the subject covered by Luke in Acts 15. Specifically, this may refer to a private meeting with some apostles and church leaders just before the council officially convened in AD 49. According to Luke, the Jerusalem Council was organized specifically to address those in the church who insisted that "Unless you keep the ancient Jewish custom of circumcision taught by Moses, you cannot be saved" (Acts 15:1). As you can see, this was the same false gospel that was contaminating the churches in Galatia. Presiding over the Council was James, the brother of Christ, who served as the bishop of Jerusalem at that time.

Interestingly, this passage gives us a clue to when Paul's conversion took place. If we start with AD 49 (the year he revisited Jerusalem) and subtract fourteen years (the time since his first visit), we get the year AD 35. We know that Paul was saved three years prior to his first visit (Gal 1:18), which puts his conversion at around AD 32. If that were the case, then Paul's dramatic encounter with Jesus would have taken place not too long after the resurrection of Christ and the birth of the early church on the day of Pentecost. Apparently, Paul did not waste any time persecuting the church while it was still young. More importantly, God did not waste any time calling him to an apostolic ministry.

One of the distinguishing traits of Paul's ministry is that he rarely traveled alone. In this particular instance, he is accompanied by Barnabas and Titus. Barnabas is one of the most endearing characters in the New Testament. His real name was Joseph, but the apostles gave him the nickname Barnabas (meaning "Son of Encouragement," as seen in Acts 4:36), apparently because he had such a supportive spirit and had a knack for helping people succeed in the work of the Lord. Paul was one such beneficiary of this wonderful ministry. It was Barnabas who convinced the apostles that Paul's conversion was authentic (Acts 9:27). He was also with Paul during the latter's first missionary journey (Acts 13). Undoubtedly, Paul mentions Barnabas in this letter with much fondness and gratitude. There is no question that Paul's ministry was enriched because of Barnabas' special ministry of encouragement. We are fortunate indeed if we have such a person in our lives.

Then there is Titus. The New Testament epistle that bears his name is testimony of how important Titus was to Paul. Although Titus is not mentioned at all in the book of Acts, we find enough information in other epistles to assemble a reasonably vivid portrait of this young soldier of Christ. Paul refers to Titus as his child in faith (Titus 1:4), which suggests that Paul was instrumental in his conversion and subsequent training in ministry. Titus is perhaps best known for his ministry in Crete, where he served as bishop. Crete is also where Titus remained throughout his ministry, since it is believed that he died and was buried there. It is noteworthy that Titus was an uncircumcised Gentile, a fact that will prove relevant to Paul's thesis regarding the Galatian controversy.

Paul stated that he returned to Jerusalem in order to meet with the apostles based there. Paul's goal was to make sure they were in full agreement on their stand against the false teachings of the Judaizers. In his mind, failure to reach an agreement would undermine all they had accomplished up until this moment. It would certainly have been a shame if all the effort they invested in winning lost souls and planting fissional churches would crumble at the hands of legalistic zealots who did not have the best interest of God's kingdom in mind.

Paul's Detractors Overruled

Even though Paul had many critics, he was blessed to have the support of the right people. Speaking of the Jerusalem apostles, he said,

> And they supported me and did not even demand that my companion Titus be circumcised, though he was a Gentile. Even that question came up only because of some so-called Christians there—false ones, really—who were secretly brought in. They sneaked in to spy on us and take away the freedom we have in Christ Jesus. They wanted to enslave us and force us to follow their Jewish regulations. (Gal 2:3-4)

The presence of Titus, an uncircumcised Gentile convert, could have threatened the cause of Paul. The Judaizers could have made a big deal about this and demanded that the young apprentice be circumcised in order to attain full covenantal status in God's kingdom. And worse, what if the leaders in Jerusalem sided with the Judaizers just to avoid any trouble? Imagine then how relieved Paul was when the Jerusalem apostles looked at Titus and did not insist that he be circumcised. This single gesture assured Paul that he had the full cooperation of the church leadership on the issue they were about to debate. Having the right people on your side is a great encouragement when we contend for the truth. We can see that God was certainly taking care of his church at this crucial stage of history.

Why did the matter of Titus' circumcision even come up? It appears that reinforcement was brought in by the opposition in order to stir up trouble for Paul. These troublemakers are described as "spies," an interesting word choice because it implies someone planted in a camp for the purpose of a military takeover. Paul's language demonstrates that this controversy was tantamount to an ecclesiastical war designed to undermine the work of the church. Such a serious matter had to be dealt with head-on.

It's an old political ploy that desperate people still use today. For some reason, troublemakers just don't know how to leave things alone. Instead, they get into the middle of the action and bring in as many as they can in order to beef up their position with a strong show of force. Paul describes the malicious nature of their plot as something done "secretly." This means that even before the meeting took place, false teachers had already met and planned out how they were going to subvert the ministry of Paul and those on his side. It is sad to see such manipulative schemes still taking place today. It is even more upsetting to see it happening in the church. But God will not be mocked. I firmly believe that no matter what opposition we face, if we are on the side of truth, the Lord will cover us with a hedge of protection so that even the gates of hell itself will not prevail against us.

The false teachers in Jerusalem had one motive for their actions—to enslave people with unnecessary religious demands. Such demands simply chip away at the core of the gospel because they undermine the redemptive work of Christ at Calvary's cross. The death of Christ was a gift of God designed to rid us of the guilt of our sins and liberate us from sin's consequences.

It is puzzling then to consider why the Judaizers would want people to return to the very way of life that once bound them in the chains of religiosity. The Jewish regulations had no power to save, yet the false teachers insisted that Gentile converts be bound to them for no good reason other than the desire to lord their will over others. We ought to watch out for power-hungry wolves who presume to lead us with their profound religious knowledge but are not committed to the saving and liberating power of the true gospel of Jesus Christ.

Paul calls these wolves "so-called Christians." They carry the label of Christ and deceptively dress the part of a godly leader. But their hearts are far from God, and the Lord will have no part with them or their fiendish schemes. This is an appropriate reminder that not every person who calls himself a Christian is truly a follower of Christ. In today's culture, "Christian" can sometimes be nothing more than a label that one puts on whenever it seems convenient to do so. But the true evidence of one's faith is in behavior and lifestyle. As James said, "It isn't enough just to have faith . . . Faith that doesn't show itself by good deeds is no faith at all—it is dead and useless" (Jas 2:17).

I once had a conversation with a woman who found out I was a pastor. She then told me she was also a churchgoing individual. When I asked her, "So how long have you been a follower of Christ?" I was surprised by her reply. She said, "Well, I just attend church, but I wouldn't exactly describe myself as a follower of Jesus." It just goes to show that behaving religiously does not make you a true disciple. One must believe and behave according to the gospel in order to be a true Christian, a devoted follower of Jesus Christ.

In contrast to the wicked motives of the false teachers, Paul had a pure motive in standing his ground for the truth. In spite of all the efforts to undermine his ministry, he said, "But we refused to give in to them for a single moment. We wanted to preserve the truth of the gospel message for you" (Gak 2:5). He was not alone, for he had the full support of the church leadership in defying the work of the enemy. Their refusal to give in to the pressure of the Judaizers benefited not only the believers in the early church, but also those of us who follow Christ today. Because of their steadfastness, the gospel message is preserved and the truth that sets people free continues to be preached by those who remain fully committed to Christ and his kingdom.

Paul's Ministry Affirmed

If you stand for what is true, it is important to stick with your convictions whether or not anyone else agrees with you. However, there is something special about having people you love and respect coming alongside you and affirming what you stand for. We are, after all, only human, and we could use all the support we can get, especially if it is from the right crowd.

Paul was blessed with such an affirmation. He did not long for it, but God, in his wisdom, provided it anyway. The apostle said to the Galatians,

> And the leaders of the church had nothing to add to what I was preaching (By the way, their reputation as great leaders made no difference to me, for God has no favorites). Instead, they saw that God had given me the responsibility of preaching the gospel to the Gentiles, just as he had given Peter the responsibility of preaching to the Jews. For the same God who worked through Peter as the apostle to the Jews also worked through me as the apostle to the Gentiles. (Gal 2:6-8)

In the ancient world, the opinion of a person of authority was considered more valuable than the opinion of a subordinate. Of course, the same principle can still hold true today—albeit to a lesser degree. In a sense, the Jerusalem apostles could be viewed as Paul's superiors because they were appointed first. Now, for Paul, the matter of apostolic superiority was neither here nor there, for he states that their reputation as great leaders had no influence on his position regarding the truth. In fact, there is a hint of hesitation in Paul's tone regarding his opinion of the Jerusalem apostles. Some have suggested that a few of the apostles may have actually pressured Paul to ease up on his position so as not to rock the boat once the Jerusalem Council was to convene. Fortunately, Paul's argument in defense of the gospel (during their private meeting) was so solid that all the apostles were eventually won to his side. If this is true, then it is easy to understand why Paul might have been a little irked (and therefore weary) with how some of the "respectable" apostles behaved. If anything, this would have convinced Paul all the more to seek only the approval of God because the approval of men, no matter how flattering, is ultimately fleeting and unimportant.

But for the Galatian reader, the opinions of the original apostles may have been an important matter, especially since the false teachers were casting a shadow of doubt on the legitimacy of Paul's ministry. To remove all doubt, Paul tells his readers that the message he preached was so pure and complete that the Jerusalem leaders had nothing to add to it—a striking indictment against the false teachers who wanted to add unnecessary demands on the gospel.

When Paul first visited Jerusalem three years after his conversion, many were skeptical about the authenticity of his newfound faith. The Bible says, "When Saul arrived in Jerusalem, he tried to meet with the believers, but they were all afraid of him. They thought he was only pretending to be a believer!" (Acts 9:26). At that time, their fear was warranted, considering Paul's reputation as a persecutor and enemy of the Christian church. However, fourteen years later, there was no longer any doubt regarding his conversion and call. The leaders of Jerusalem fully recognized that Paul was uniquely commissioned by Christ to preach the gospel to the Gentiles. The phrase "they saw" (Gal 2:7) is literally rendered "they came to see," meaning that they became convinced by intently scrutinizing the life and ministry of Paul. In fact, Paul puts himself on equal standing with Peter by describing how his calling paralleled that of the "senior" apostle. His "just as" statements—that he was called just as Peter was and that it was the same God who called them—were meant to debunk the claim by false teachers that Paul was not to be received as a true apostle of Jesus Christ.

In the church today, there are those who are overly obsessed with titles and ranks. It is indicative of a culture that seeks the approval of people before taking a stand. It plagues modern politicians who conduct field polls prior to taking a position on controversial issues. People like this cannot be trusted. They play on people's emotions as a manipulative trick designed for personal gain. Paul, in his letter to Timothy, warns us about such people. He said, "For a time is coming when people will no longer listen to right teaching. They will follow their own desires and will look for teachers who will tell them whatever they want to hear. They will reject the truth and follow strange myths" (2 Tim 4:3–4).

God does not play favorites. He is not impressed with our eloquence or our worldly achievements. He will approve of us simply on the basis of what is right and true. So the question is never "Is God on our side?" Rather, we ought to ask ourselves if we are on the side of God. Paul was certainly convinced that he was.

Paul's Apostleship Recognized

In affirming the authenticity of Paul's conversion and call, the apostles in Jerusalem officially endorsed the apostolic ministry of Paul among the Gentiles. Paul said,

> In fact, James, Peter, and John, who were known as pillars of the church, recognized the gift God had given me, and they accepted Barnabas and me as their co-workers. They encouraged us to keep preaching to the Gentiles, while they continued their work with the Jews. Their only suggestion was that we keep on helping the poor, which I have always been eager to do. (Gal 2:9–10)

That Paul specifically mentioned James, Peter, and John indicates that these three men were among the most prominent leaders of the church in Jerusalem. Interestingly, James is mentioned even before Peter and John. For even though Peter and John were more senior apostles in terms of when they were called, James had a more senior role in that he was the appointed bishop over the church in Jerusalem, as attested by his presiding role during the Jerusalem Council. Paul referred to these three men as "pillars of the church," showing that they had an important role in the formation of the New Testament Church. Paul would later expound on this concept in his letter to the church in Ephesus where he wrote, "We are his house, built on the foundation of the apostles and the prophets. And the cornerstone is Christ Jesus himself" (Eph 2:20). We are all parts of one body with Christ as our head. As leader of the church, Christ alone deserves to be worshiped and praised. But Paul also understood the rightful place of apostles in the kingdom of God and reminded believers to bestow honor and respect upon those who work hard to lead the church with integrity. He even said to the Thessalonians,

> Dear brothers and sisters, honor those who are your leaders in the Lord's work. They work hard among you and warn you against all that is wrong. Think highly of them and give them your wholehearted love because of their work. And remember to live peaceably with each other. (1 Thess 5:12–13)

The endorsement of Paul's ministry marks a special time in the history of the church because it was the catalyst to the global missionary work foretold by Christ, who said that the Christian witness would reach Jerusalem, Judea, Samaria, and the ends of the earth (Acts 1:8). Paul and the rest of the apostles were equal in terms of their place in the work of God's kingdom; hence, they are all coworkers. What makes each apostle unique is the specific locus of their calling. In the case of the early church, many of the original apostles were called to evangelize the Jews, whereas Paul was called to evangelize the Gentile world. Both callings are equally valuable to the mission of the church.

Churches today will do well to learn this lesson. We are not each other's competition; rather, we are all members of the same team who are each given a unique role. There is no place for jealousy in the ministry, for we will each be accountable for accomplishing what we are specifically called to do. Someone once wisely reminded me that it will take all kinds of evangelists to win all kinds of people for Christ.

Though the apostles had nothing to add to the message of Paul, they encouraged him to be mindful of the poor no matter where God would send him. Paul, of course, was more than happy to oblige, since he had already incorporated this practice in his apostolic ministry. According to Scripture, Paul helped the poor in Jerusalem during a time of famine (Acts 11:27–30), he collected money from the various Gentile churches to help the Jerusalem poor (Acts 24:17), he took a collection in Greece to help Christians in Jerusalem who were going through tough times (Rom 15:26), he instructed the Corinthians to help the Christians in Jerusalem the same way the Galatians did (1 Cor 16:1–4), and he praised the Macedonians for their sacrificial giving on behalf of the suffering Christians in Jerusalem (2 Cor 8:1–5). So it is clear that when Paul promised the apostles to remember the poor, he was not just offering them lip service but was indeed very serious about the biblical mandate to take care of those in need.

The Christian church, being an institution of humans, has made many mistakes in its two-thousand-year history. Things have been done in the name of Christ that we are certainly not proud of. But the church's legacy of caring for the poor is deeply rooted in history. In fact, the benevolent ministries of the Christian church—orphanages, hospitals, feeding centers, calamity response teams, and the like—remain one of the most powerful manifestations of how the love of God is demonstrated to the world. Jesus said that we will always have the poor among us (John 12:8). May we never falter to live up to our God-given responsibility to care for those who are not able to care for themselves.

There is no limit to what the church can accomplish when it aligns itself with the truth of God. In one of the most memorable scenes in the epic film *Gladiator*, Maximus and a few other men were in the center of a massive coliseum surrounded by some of the best warriors of Rome. The men feared they did not stand a chance against such fierce and skilled combatants. Maximus ordered the men into formation and reminded them that no matter what happened, they were to fight as one rather than as individuals—united in their goal to defeat the Roman soldiers. When the battle was over, the lifeless bodies of the Roman soldiers blanketed the coliseum as the shocked emperor watched in disbelief. How could have such a raggedy group of second-rate fighters defeat Rome's finest? Simple. They were all in agreement and fought for their lives as a cohesive unit. In the end, unity won.

As believers, we are constantly at war with God's enemies. As the attacks come from every side, we are too often overwhelmed with feelings of helplessness and fear of inevitable defeat. Let us not forget, however, that we were not meant to fight for the truth all on our own. God has given us other people to strive alongside us. And just as Peter and Paul were different in their personalities, styles, and approaches to ministry, we too will find that our coworkers in ministry are often noticeably different from ourselves. But we are colleagues nonetheless. And in times of crisis, we soon realize that the enemies of our enemies are really our friends. If we are committed to the same truth of the one and only gospel, then we ought to learn how to work in agreement with one another. On that matter, those of us who believe can certainly get along.

4

Peter, Peter, Kosher Eater
Galatians 2:11–21

THERE'S NOTHING LIKE SHARING a wonderful meal with people whose company you enjoy. I'm no racist, but I have a particular fondness for eating with Filipinos. Of course, the fact that I grew up in the Philippines has a lot to do with that. To me, Filipinos are familiar people. I know what makes them laugh, I understand them when they speak Taglish (a combination of Tagalog, a local dialect, and English), and I can identify the ingredients in the food no matter how exotic they might seem to others. In this case, familiarity breeds comfort.

Every now and then, however, we are thrust into a culture markedly different from our own. When I was in seminary, my roommate from India invited me to spend one spring vacation with his family in Florida. I immediately obliged; after all, how can you resist the opportunity to claim that you were in Fort Lauderdale for spring break? As wonderful as the host family was, I was a little intimidated during mealtimes. The food on the table was not familiar, and we ate with our hands. (Most people think that Filipinos also eat with their hands, but after that experience, I realized that Filipinos eat with their fingers while Indians eat with their hands.) However, the longer I stayed with this lovely family, the more comfortable I became spending time with them and eating their food. In fact, by the end of my stay, despite the fact that I was experiencing curry overload, I was thoroughly enjoying myself and wished I didn't have to return to school.

Two thousand years ago, the Apostle Peter had a similar experience. As a Jewish man, he would have been most comfortable with Jewish people. I'm fairly certain he favored kosher meals. But one day, God interfered with his life in a way that would force him out of his comfort zone.

God was setting the scene for Peter to share the gospel to non-Jews. Knowing that Peter, a devout Jew, might resist the idea of bringing the gospel to Gentiles, the Lord gave Peter a vision. According to Luke's account,

> Peter went up to the flat roof to pray. It was about noon, and he was hungry. But while lunch was being prepared, he fell into a trance. He saw the sky open, and something like a large sheet was let down by its four corners. In the sheet were all sorts of animals, reptiles, and birds. Then a voice said to him, "Get up, Peter; kill and eat them." "Never, Lord," Peter declared. "I have never in all my life eaten anything forbidden by our Jewish laws." The voice spoke again, "If God says something is acceptable, don't say it isn't." The same vision was repeated three times. Then the sheet was pulled up again to heaven. (Acts 10:9–16)

The shock value of this vision, along with the fact that it was given to Peter three times, indicates that God was adamant about his desire for the gospel to be shared with those who were otherwise considered *unclean* by the standards of Judaism. It seems as if religious dogmatists tend to obsess over avoiding the unclean, while God is more concerned about transforming what is unclean. The message of redemption is for all who are willing to believe that the blood of Christ is able to cover our sins and wash them all away.

Shortly after this eye-opening incident, Peter was invited to the home of a Gentile named Cornelius. In Cornelius' house, Peter preached the gospel, and the salvation of God came upon the entire household, marking a new chapter in the mission of the church. The gospel was no longer limited to the people in the Jewish community. The message of Christ's death and resurrection, along with the ensuing gift of salvation, was shown to be for all people—regardless of whether or not they were circumcised Jews.

Even though Peter was primarily called to minister to the Jews, this experience prepared him for fellowship among Gentiles. It seems this part of the story should end with "And they lived happily ever after." However, in this particular instance, something went horribly wrong. Peter, the great pillar of the church, did something that had the potential to jeopardize the mission of the church among the Gentiles. For this reason, Paul had to step in to deal with the problem. In this portion of his letter to the Galatians, Paul explains exactly what took place.

Showdown in Antioch

Paul doesn't mince words when describing what Peter did wrong. He writes,

> But when Peter came to Antioch, I had to oppose him to his face, for what he did was very wrong. When he first arrived, he ate with the Gentile Christians who were not circumcised. But afterward, when some friends of James came, Peter wouldn't eat with the Gentiles anymore. He was afraid of criticism from these people who insisted on the necessity of circumcision. (Gal 2:11–12)

Apparently, Paul went on to minister in Antioch sometime after attending the First Council of Jerusalem. Antioch was an important city for the early church. Founded by Seleucus Nicator in 300 BC, it was named Antioch on the Orontes to differentiate it from the many other cities that were also named Antioch. Third only to Rome and Alexandria, it had a significant population of half a million people, many of whom were Jewish immigrants. Furthermore, Jewish Christians settled in Antioch to escape the persecution marked by the martyrdom of Stephen. Those believers evangelized the Jewish community there, while other believers from Cyprus and Cyrene preached the gospel to the Gentiles. As a result, Antioch had one of the first successful cross-cultural churches in the first century. Also noteworthy is the fact that the term "Christian" was first used to describe believers in that city (Acts 11:19–26).

Antioch was particularly important to the ministry of Paul. He established his headquarters there for a full year. In fact, all three of Paul's missionary journeys were launched from Antioch. And keeping with Paul's promise to care for the poor, the believers in Antioch were fully committed to providing relief for the poor in Jerusalem and Judea.

At some point, the Apostle Peter had an opportunity to visit this thriving, model church. Because the church was a culturally diverse congregation, Jews and Gentiles ate in fellowship with each other regularly. This means the Jewish believers there consciously ignored the religious stipulations against eating with non-Jews. Peter, therefore, gladly ate with the Gentiles upon his arrival.

However, a group of Judaizers from Jerusalem soon came to Antioch. Upon hearing that Peter fellowshipped with uncircumcised Gentiles, they chastised him for doing so. Apparently, they used their friendship with James as leverage for putting pressure on him. (By the way, the text does not say that James actually condoned the behavior of his "friends," as this may be a classic case of name-dropping.) Not wanting to stir up any controversies and fearful of being criticized by the people from Jerusalem, Peter backed off and ceased to eat with the Gentiles in Antioch.

Some have wondered why a big deal is made about Peter's actions. After all, wasn't he just trying to keep the peace and preserve order for the early church? If someone other than Peter committed this faux pas, perhaps it could have been overlooked as a minor infraction with no bearing on the health of the Christian church. But we are talking about Peter—an original follower of Jesus Christ and a pillar of the church! Furthermore, Peter is far more accountable for his actions because it was he who received the vision regarding God's acceptance of the previously *unclean* Gentiles. If anything, Peter should have used this opportunity to rebuke the men from Jerusalem for being enslaved to their religiosity and for attempting to sabotage the mission of the church among the Gentiles.

Peter was guilty of two serious offenses for any church leader—racism and cowardice. By distancing himself from the Gentiles, he was being racist because his actions suggested that he, as a Jew, was not fit for fellowship with Gentiles because they were an inferior class of people. Yet doesn't the gospel of Christ dispose of such absurdities? Are we not all equal at the foot of the cross? Peter's behavior was a grave betrayal of the very gospel he was supposed to uphold.

Furthermore, Peter acted cowardly because, as a recognized leader of the church, he failed to lead. And why was he afraid to lead? He was concerned about criticism from others. Let's get one thing straight: If you are called to leadership, you had better get used to being criticized; it simply comes with the territory. More importantly, criticism, while sometimes helpful, should never be a determining factor in the choice to stand for what is right and true. As a pillar of the church, so much was resting on Peter that if this matter had not been dealt with, the body of Christ would have suffered a tremendous blow. We don't always understand why God calls ordinary people to such positions of responsibility, but if you are indeed called to leadership, then by all means you must lead!

Now, we are not saying that Peter was facing an artificial struggle. The dilemma was real, make no mistake. Even today, we must ask ourselves how we are to best minister within a given culture. However, culture must be subservient to truth. As a missiological principle, wherever culture does not violate the truth of Scripture, it ought to be left alone. But when an aspect of culture is at odds with the clear teachings of Scripture, it must be challenged and ultimately changed. In this case, the cultural practice of circumcision and adherence to Jewish law was not in and of itself wrong.

But because these were not prerequisites to faith in Christ, it was wrong to insist that an uncircumcised person was in any way lesser.

Equally significant is the influence of Peter as a chief disciple. Because he was a recognized leader of the church, his action served as a cue for how other believers were to behave. In this case, his misdeeds gave way to others also behaving badly. As Paul recalls, "As a result, other Jewish Christians followed Peter's hypocrisy, and even Barnabas was led astray by their hypocrisy" (Gal 2:13).

The charge of hypocrisy is as harsh as it sounds. The word "hypocrite" describes someone who is two-faced. It is derived from a Greek term for a theatrical mask. In modern times, actors show emotion and character through facial expression. But in ancient times, thespians used a variety of masks to display a particular character. Conceivably, a performer could be wearing a mask bearing a sad face when in fact his real face could be sporting a wide smile. So in this sense, he has two faces, hence the term. In the case of Peter, his two faces were the one he showed the Gentile converts when fellowshipping with them and the one he showed the Judaizers when they accused him of betraying their religious values. Peter's hypocrisy was so far-reaching that it even influenced Barnabas himself. Who would have ever imagined that he, the great encourager, would himself be encouraged to do something so wrong?

A leader's conduct is never inconsequential. When a leader does what is right, the church is built up; when a leader does what is wrong, the church suffers. For this reason, Paul had no choice but to confront Peter and rectify the matter.

The Heart of the Matter

Paul must have been livid when he heard about what Peter did. His anger would have been exacerbated by the negative influence Peter had on the other believers. He explained his reaction to the Galatians, saying, "When I saw that they were not following the truth of the gospel message, I said to Peter in front of all the others . . ." (Gal 2:14a). It should be noted that Paul is clear about his motive for correcting Peter. This was not a personal vendetta against Peter, nor was there any hint of resentment or jealousy over any previous altercation.

Paul's concern was as it always had been: the preservation of the gospel's truth. Specifically, he wanted to preserve the idea that those who believe in Christ, whether Jew or Gentile, are all equal members of the kingdom of God. Therefore, there is no acceptable reason for segregating Jews and Gentiles in times of table fellowship. Peter's conduct was a betrayal of this most important principle.

In ancient Jewish culture, one was encouraged to rebuke a person in private. It was deemed the kind thing to do and kept the offending party from unnecessary embarrassment. However, in this case, Paul felt that it was necessary to rebuke Peter *in front of all the others*. The potentially devastating consequences of Peter's offense made it necessary to confront him publicly. This may not have been how Paul preferred to go about it, as he surely found no pleasure in exposing Peter in the open. But for the overall good of the church, and because of Peter's position of authority, Paul was left with no other choice. Such a public offense required an equally public rebuke. Jesus himself once said, "But people who are not aware that they are doing wrong will be punished only lightly. Much is required from those to whom much is given, and much more is required from those to whom much more is given" (Luke 12:48). Because of Peter's role as a senior leader in the early church, it was only right that he was held to a higher standard of accountability.

Accusing his ministry colleague of hypocrisy, Paul explained to Peter, "Since you, a Jew by birth, have discarded the Jewish laws and are living like a Gentile, why are you now trying to make these Gentiles follow the Jewish traditions. You and I are Jews by birth, not 'sinners' like the Gentiles" (Gal 2:14b–15a). As if he were shaking his head in disbelief, Paul tells Peter that his actions just didn't make any sense. That is, if Peter really believed, as he and the other apostles affirmed in the First Council of Jerusalem, that he was free from the demands of the old covenant, then why was he requiring the Gentiles to be subject to the very laws he no longer lived under? The hypocrisy of Peter was not only blatant, it was also void of any justification.

Against the backdrop of such senselessness, Paul clarifies why it was reasonable to expect Peter to behave differently. He writes,

> You and I are Jews by birth, not "sinners" like the Gentiles. Yet we know that a person is made right with God by faith in Jesus Christ, not by obeying the law. And we have believed in Christ Jesus, so that we might be made right with God because of our faith in Christ, not because we have obeyed the law. For no one will ever be made right with God by obeying the law. (Gal 2:15b–16)

This passage is the most theologically significant portion of the entire book of Galatians. Here, we find Paul's doctrinal thesis, which serves as a response to the Galatian controversy. This great doctrine of justification is so central to the message of the gospel that Paul so adamantly seeks to defend. Amusingly, the letter to the Galatians has sometimes been dubbed "Little Romans" because both epistles share the doctrine of justification as its central theme.

Interestingly, some people believed that Gentiles were born under a curse of sin from which Jews were spared; hence, they viewed Gentiles as *sinners*, even though the Bible makes it clear that all have sinned (Rom 3:23). Paul addresses this misconception by making it clear that justification is not a birthright; rather, it is a result of having faith in Christ. Case in point? Both Peter and Paul were born as Jews, yet that was not the reason they were justified.

Justification is a forensic term that so aptly describes the effects of Christ's redemptive work. It literally means "to declare to be right." Simply put, it is the opposite of being tried in court and found guilty. Justification deals with the issue of righteousness, or having a right standing in the eyes of a just God. But this proposition poses a serious problem. One of my first theology professors, Dr. D. C. Barnes, framed it for me this way: "How can a perfectly just God justify the unjust and remain Just and Justifier, when in view of divine justice, the unjust have no credentials by which to merit justification?" Read that again about three or four times and you will realize it is not as confusing as it initially sounds. Barnes is simply asking how God can legally declare a guilty sinner as "not guilty" without damaging his own status as a Just Judge.

Suppose you go to the local courthouse and watch a murder trial. After weeks of hearing the evidence, the jury deliberates on the merits of the case and eventually decides the accused is guilty beyond the shadow of a doubt. Suddenly, the judge, completely ignoring the verdict, says to the murderer, "I know the jury determined that you are guilty, but I'm in a good mood today so I'm declaring you not guilty, and you are free to go." While the judge is certainly capable of speaking those words, doing so would damage his or her reputation as a just person. The judge would, in effect, no longer be just. In fact, every one of us would consider such a person an unfit judge.

The same is true (if not more true) for God. Even though it would be nice if he were to set all sinners free on the basis of sheer kindness, his attribute of justice prevents this from happening without any just cause. So now we are back to the original question: How does God manage to justify us if we are sinners? The answer is found in the person of Jesus Christ.

Christ, by his death, satisfied the demands of the law and made restitution for sin on behalf of us sinners. If we then, with no regard to our race or religion, put our faith in Christ and believe that he died in our place, the righteousness of Jesus is imputed (i.e., credited) to our account. This is why Paul can say we are justified not by obeying the law but by faith in Jesus Christ.

What, then, is the purpose of the law? The law makes us aware of our sin but has no power to cleanse us from it. It is like looking into a mirror and discovering we have an ink stain on our forehead. The mirror can bring awareness of our stain, but it is not capable of removing it. For that you need soap, water, and a towel. Likewise, the Jewish law was helpful in making us aware of how unrighteous we are, but only the blood of Christ can cover up our sin and wash it away completely. This act of cleansing takes effect in our lives whenever we respond with belief. Thus, we are saved by grace (Christ's gift of redemption) through faith (trusting in Christ to be our Savior).

Peter preached this very message as an apostle, which is why Paul found it remarkable that he would betray this gospel truth. Paul's rebuke was therefore not only reasonable, but also fully warranted. Also, it would leave the Galatian reader with no other recourse but to reject the false teachers who were leading them astray with their false gospel.

The Theological Rationale

As Paul lays the doctrinal foundation for his argument, he anticipates a counter-argument from his opponents, particularly those opponents who are wary of anyone who might take the position of an *antinomian*. This term, coined by Martin Luther in the sixteenth century, comes from a combination of two Greek words: *anti*, meaning "against," and *nomos*, meaning "law." It describes those who believe that the law no longer applies to them. Unfortunately, they tend to live out their freedom from the law by taking it to the other extreme; that is, since they are no longer under the law, they are now free to do whatever they wish (resulting in chaotic lawlessness).

Predicting such a response from some of his critics, Paul writes, "But suppose we seek to be made right with God through faith in Christ and then are found guilty because we have abandoned the law. Would that mean Christ has led us into sin? Absolutely not!" (Gal 2:17). As you can see, one might argue that if we are no longer under the law, then we can live as we please, even if that means living a sinful lifestyle. And if freedom in Christ is the cause of such liberty, then Christ himself would be culpable for such an evil way of living. Paul, however, is quick to clarify that one who lives in sin because of his freedom in Christ is completely missing the point of Christian liberty. So he goes on to explain, "Rather, I am a sinner if I rebuild the old system of law I already tore down. For when I tried to keep the law, it condemned me. So I died to the law—I stopped trying to meet all its requirements—so that I might live for God" (Gal 2:18–19).

Paul illustrated his point by presenting a hypothetical, although somewhat autobiographical, scenario. He speaks of a sinner who has given up trying to live up to the standards of the law because he realizes it can never be done. It doesn't mean that he is not able to do any good at all but rather that he is not capable of obeying the law in its entirety. The Bible makes it clear that to be guilty of one sin is to be guilty of defying all the law. Take, for instance, a chandelier hanging from the ceiling by chain links. How many links have to break before it comes crashing to the ground? Seven? Twelve? Three? No, only one! Just one broken link is all it takes for the chandelier to shatter into pieces. Likewise, even if we don't break every stipulation in the law, we are guilty of violating the entire law because, in one way or another, all have sinned.

All the law is able to do is condemn the unrighteous person by exposing our sinfulness and inability to save ourselves. Salvation comes only when we each surrender our life to Christ and chooses to live for God by faith. For Paul, it doesn't make sense for such a person, saved by grace, to go back to his or her old way of life, which never worked to begin with. Instead, a person saved by grace should continue to live by grace, since the previous method of living has already been destroyed. More importantly, living by grace does not mean doing whatever we want. Instead, it means we are now free to live as we were originally expected to.

Let me put it this way. If a person commits a crime by breaking the law, he or she is put in jail as punishment for that act. But suppose an advocate, by an act of kindness, satisfies the requirements of the criminal's sentence, thereby muting his or her punishment. Is this person now free to start committing new crimes? Absolutely not! Doing so would result in being sent back to prison. Rather than return to a life of crime, he or she must use that newfound freedom to start living a decent and productive life, because this is how that person should have been living in the first place. Liberty is not a catalyst to behave badly once again; it is a motivation to live justly because the saved person is fully grateful for the grace bestowed upon him or her.

In his letter to the Corinthians, Paul said, "Anyone who belongs to Christ has become a new person. The old life is gone; a new life has begun!" (2 Cor 5:17). Paul wrote this out of his own experience. How else can you explain a Christ-hating persecutor becoming one of the chief advocates for the Christian gospel? Such a transformation can only be the work of God. It is fitting then that this life be lived for his glory.

Implications for All Who Believe

Paul ends this section of the letter by making a few practical applications for both himself and his readers. Theology, after all, is of little value until we learn how to put right ideas into practice. The Bible reminds us that we are to be doers of the Word and not hearers only (Jas 1:22). So in light of the fact that the redemptive grace of God makes us new creatures, Paul writes, "My old self has been crucified with Christ. It is no longer I who live, but Christ lives in me. So I live in this earthly body by trusting in the Son of God, who loved me and gave himself for me" (Gal 2:20).

Here, as in other Pauline epistles, we are introduced to the notion of being *in Christ*. How does one begin to live in Christ? It starts by allowing our old selves to die. Our old selves, our sinful ways of life, must be laid bare at the cross of Christ and put to death. Only then can our new selves be born. Jesus once said, "Unless a kernel of wheat is planted in the soil and dies, it remains alone . . . But its death will produce many new kernels—a plentiful harvest of new lives" (John 12:24). This principle of life through death also applies to our redemption. We cannot be alive in Christ unless we are first dead to the world. But once we are alive in Christ, we enter into solidarity *with him* that our existence is best described as being *in him*; hence, we are now *in Christ*.

Having died to his old self, Paul can now describe his present existence as Christ living in him. While he remains the same on the outside, the self that animates his body is no longer the old Paul that used to live in rebellion against God. We surrender our lives to Christ only to discover that he takes no prisoners. Instead, he puts us to death and, in place of our old lives, gives us new and everlasting life. So those who trust in the Lord, though they continue to exist in the flesh, now live according to the loving and gracious gift of new life in Christ.

Most of us are notorious for taking gifts for granted. When I was a child, there was a popular Japanese animated show called *Voltes V*. It was about a robot that was actually made up of five different spacecrafts that would join together electro-magnetically to form one unit. In the true spirit of capitalism, a company made a toy version of this robot—and I wanted one! For months I begged and hinted to my parents. Then came Christmas of 1978. Under the tree was a box that seemed to be just the right shape. I lifted it, and it was just the right weight. Could this be the toy I wanted? I could only wait and hope. Soon enough, it was time to open my gift. There it was (cue angelic voices)—my very own *Voltes V* toy! I was determined to cherish it forever. Needless to say, it didn't take too long before the toy lost its appeal, and a few years later, it was retired to the box of old toys. I don't even remember where it ultimately ended up. So much for cherishing my gift forever.

The gift of God, his amazing grace, should never be taken for granted. Paul reminded the Galatians, "I do not treat the grace of God as meaningless. For if keeping the law could make us right with God, then there was no need for Christ to die" (Gal 2:21). Salvation is not a fad toy designed to keep us amused for the moment. It is a present that came at such a great cost—the life of God's only begotten Son. And how do we cherish this most amazing gift? By receiving it wholeheartedly by faith and living this new life for the sake of the one who laid down his life for us.

Furthermore, Paul stresses the value of this gift by letting us know there is none like it. Once again challenging the flawed thinking of the false teachers, he argues that the death of Christ would have been a useless, and therefore foolish, act if there were any other way to obtain righteousness. But as is stands, our only hope for salvation is the redemptive death of Christ at Calvary. There was no other way, and Christ is our only hope.

So many people today live with the same mindset as the false teachers. They think they can bypass the importance of the cross and attain righteousness some other way. Some do it through church membership, acts of kindness, moral living, making a pilgrimage to a holy site, or obeying the Ten Commandments. Some might even think that being born of a particular race or religion is all it takes to be justified. The list of *fig leaves* is simply endless. But those who think that way should consider one thing: If their fig leaf were sufficient for the attainment of righteousness and a right standing with God, then for what reason did God send his one and only Son? Why did he bother asking Christ to give up his life and die on the cross? When we seek to be righteous in any other way apart from faith in Jesus, we make a mockery of God's redemptive plan.

It is little wonder, therefore, that Paul went out of his way to rebuke Peter in public. Furthermore, this confrontation provides a number of lessons that the modern church must heed. First, there is no such thing as a perfect leader. Peter's imperfections were obvious from the first time we meet him in the gospels. He had an impulsive personality with a sharp tongue to boot. Even as a pillar apostle, he is not spared from making mistakes. But before we judge Peter too harshly, let us remember that every one of us is capable of such failings.

Second, no leader, regardless of title or position, is above criticism and correction. Being challenged and corrected come with the territory, and skirting around this issue will only prove detrimental to our ministry. We all need someone brave enough to confront us when we are wrong. This is more difficult than it sounds. For some reason, people find it hard to confront the leaders they admire and respect. But blessed is the leader who has at least one loving person who cares enough to keep him or her straight. Apologist Ravi Zacharias makes an insightful observation on this matter. He said that one major factor in the fall of King Solomon was that he did not have a prophetic presence in his kingdom. King Saul was corrected by the prophet Samuel, and King David was corrected by the prophet Nathan, but nobody corrected King Solomon. As a result, he fell into sins such as adultery and idolatry to such startling levels that one wonders how he ever got there in the first place. Indeed, the absence of a corrective, prophetic voice would have been one major reason for this.

Third, leaders ought to adopt an attitude of humility and teachability at all times. To his credit, Peter seems to have responded positively to Paul's rebuke. He was undoubtedly humiliated by this whole episode, yet he took it like a man and used this teaching moment to mold his character, thereby making him a more effective leader in the long run.

Finally, we must have the courage to call out an injustice when we see it. Paul could have ignored Peter's offense by claiming the problem was outside of his jurisdiction. He could have also just allowed Peter to have his way in order to avoid further controversy. Yet he knew that to do so would endanger the credibility of the gospel and damage the mission of the church. We will also do well to keep the good of God's kingdom to the forefront of our thinking.

Thankfully, everyone who opens their heart to Christ and receives his gift by faith are invited to live in him and dine with him for eternity—regardless of their ethnic or cultural identity.

5

Stop! In the Name of the Law

Galatians 3:1–14

LIKE MOST PEOPLE, I find it difficult to imagine living in a land without laws. Laws, after all, help maintain peace and order in a society. However, there is only so much a law can do; it still takes people to articulate them clearly and obey them correctly. The failure to be clear and the inability to be upright renders the law ineffective and, for all practical purposes, useless.

I once heard a story that conveys this point quite amusingly. There was an American who went to the Philippines to visit a dear friend who was injured in an accident. Upon arriving, he checked in at his hotel and immediately proceeded to the hospital. Unfamiliar with the city, he walked up to a traffic cop and asked, "Excuse me, officer, can you tell me how I can get to the Philippine Orthopedic Hospital?" The cop, somewhat flustered by the unexpected question and intimidated by the notion of having to answer in English, replied, "Ahhhh, let's see . . . hmmmm . . . Oh, I know! You see this busy street?" pointing to the mad rush of cars zooming across the intersection, "Just stand in the middle of this traffic, and before you know it, you will find yourself at the Orthopedic Hospital." While the cop's answer was technically accurate, it was neither useful nor helpful. In fact, it was downright deadly. The same can be true for any directive, be it a simple set of instructions, or even the law of Moses. Correct information does not necessarily lead to upright living.

Paul's purpose in arguing against the efficacy of the law was not to devalue all laws. He simply wanted to drive home the point that the law, by itself, has no power to make a person righteous. Furthermore, to believe otherwise was not only unfortunate, but like the traffic cop's directions, it was potentially deadly.

So far, Paul has been addressing the Galatian controversy by employing an autobiographic approach. In the first and second chapters, he gave a brief description of his conversion, his visits to Jerusalem, and his confrontation with Peter. But now, in this third chapter, he applies a different approach and takes on a more doctrinal posture in his discourse. Specifically, he employs a teaching style known as a diatribe. A diatribe is characterized by a series of rhetorical questions interwoven with aggressive logical assertions. It was often used in political speeches. Even today, political advertising often takes on a diatribal tone as candidates take cheap jabs at one another. Used to an extreme, a diatribe can take the form of ranting, which isn't always effective in getting one's point across. However, this isn't the case with Paul. Although Paul is clearly forceful in this section of the letter, the objective reader will notice that he tempers his emotions with logical claims knowing that his goal is not to berate the Galatians but to defend the truth of gospel without any compromise.

In the first part of his diatribe, Paul exposes the futility of his opponent's arguments by contrasting the blessings that come by faith with the curses that result from a failure to obey the law perfectly.

The Galatians' Folly

Paul opens this section by addressing the Galatians in a way that surely got their attention. He writes, "Oh, foolish Galatians! Who has cast an evil spell on you? For the meaning of Jesus Christ's death was made clear to you as if you had seen a picture of his death on the cross" (Gal 3:1). The apostle is being very precise with his language. Normally, Paul would address believers with an endearing title such as "brothers and sisters," but here, he simply calls them "Galatians." The impersonal nature of this term is intentional.

Paul wants his readers to know that he isn't exactly fond of them at the moment. And as if that was not enough, he further describes them as "foolish." The term is used to describe someone who possesses the capacity to know what is right, yet chooses to act in a manner that is inconsistent with what is known. For instance, it is not uncommon for a parent to reprimand a child by saying, "I expected more from you because you should know better!" In the same way, Paul is clearly frustrated with the Galatians because their behavior is unjustified. How could they possibly take the side of the false teachers when they should already know the truth of the gospel? Paul is so appalled that he sarcastically asks, "Who has cast an evil spell on you?" This is a reference to the ancient practice of bewitching, in which one is hexed by a magician who seeks to influence an unsuspecting victim for ignoble reasons.

Stop! In the Name of the Law

The facetious language used in this verse is uncharacteristic for a Pauline epistle, yet it is essential to demonstrate the gravity of the Galatian controversy. There are times when it is necessary to drive home a point in such a way as to forcefully grab your audience's attention. The problem is so serious that Paul simply has no time to filter his thoughts and play nice. Moreover, his sarcasm is warranted when we take into account all the earlier efforts he had already exerted in making the gospel as plain as possible while bringing the good news to the Galatians. Paul assumes that the Galatians already possessed a lucid understanding of the gospel and all its implications. He explains, "For the meaning of Jesus' death was made as clear to you as if you had seen a picture of his death on the cross." Why is Paul able to make such an assumption? Because he himself was instrumental in introducing the Galatians to the gospel message.

In the ancient world, good communicators were characterized by the ability to paint vivid pictures by using the medium of words laid over the canvas of the mind. In today's world, technology tends to rob the modern communicator of the chance to paint such mental images. Instructional books are set aside for comic strips, and printed novels take a back seat to films. Even sermons, which a generation ago was almost completely expressed in words, are "enhanced" with skits, video clips, and PowerPoint slides. I am certainly not suggesting that any of these are wrong, but could it be that something is amiss when the preacher becomes a servant to technology rather than vice versa? Not so with Paul. As an old-school, first-century preacher, he certainly would have had a way with words. And because Paul never strayed from preaching about the crucified Christ, we have no doubt that this image was indelibly etched in the minds of the Galatians readers.

However, before we are too impressed with Paul's preaching skills, let us not forget that the secret of his preaching success was neither his eloquence, nor his theatric abilities. Surely we can never forget this episode in Paul's ministry (as told by Luke),

> On the first day of the week, we gathered with the local believers to share in the Lord's Supper. Paul was preaching to them, and since he was leaving the next day, he kept talking until midnight. The upstairs room where we met was lighted with many flickering lamps. As Paul spoke on and on, a young man named Eutychus, sitting on the windowsill, became very drowsy. Finally, he fell sound asleep and dropped three stories to his death below. (Acts 20:7–9)

Paul was such a long-winded, dare I say boring, preacher that a person actually died trying to listen to him! Perhaps I should remind you that Paul later prayed for this lad and he was brought back to life (Acts 20:10).

Paul was aware of his own shortcomings as a preacher. He confessed to the Corinthians that his preaching was "very plain" (1 Cor 2:4) and that the power of his preaching came not from "lofty words," but from the Holy Spirit. And so it is reasonable to assume that he did a good job preaching the gospel to the Galatians because the Holy Spirit was with him. What an encouragement for all those who seek to share the gospel to others. If we are led by the Spirit, we too can clearly communicate the love of Christ to those who so desperate need to hear the gospel.

A Barrage of Questions

True to the diatribe form of argumentation, Paul follows up his discussion with a series of questions. The questions are rather pointed, indicating that he is still baffled at how foolishly the Galatians have acted. These questions are also rhetorical in nature, which demonstrates that Paul clearly assumed the reader should know better because the answers to all of his questions were obvious. In general, his line of questioning is designed to indict the Galatians for their offense and ultimately to graciously restore them to a right understanding of the gospel's truth.

Paul begins his interrogation by saying, "Let me ask you this one question: Did you receive the Holy Spirit by obeying the law of Moses? Of course not! You received the Spirit because you believed the message you heard about Christ" (Gal 3:2). With this inquiry, the apostle asks his readers to return to the time when they first received the message of salvation. The way he frames the question is unique in that he focused on the Holy Spirit rather than on Christ. It is not that Christ is not important to the issue, but Paul expands the concept of salvation by showing that being saved is not simply a matter of being forgiven, for there is also the added blessing of being filled with God's Holy Spirit.

In ancient Judaism, there was a tendency to think that one earned the gift of the Spirit. For instance, if one had achieved a certain status, such as a king or a prophet, then one was fit to receive the Holy Spirit. Conversely, if that person were to act in a way as to displease God, the gift of the Holy Spirit would be removed. Take the case of King Saul. As the appointed king of Israel, he was anointed by the prophet Samuel. At that time, Samuel said to him, "the Spirit of the Lord will come powerfully upon you" (1 Sam 10:6). With this, Saul was blessed with the Spirit of God, a gift understood to be reserved only for a chosen few. Unfortunately, Saul eventually loses favor with God, and consequently, the Spirit of the Lord is taken from him (1 Sam 16:14). Even King David was mindful of this concept, so when he sinned before God, he pleaded, "Do not banish me from your presence, and don't take your Holy Spirit from me" (Ps 55:11). It is little wonder then that most Jews were under the impression that receiving (or losing) the Holy Spirit was based on human works. But by framing his question the way he did, Paul challenges this ancient notion and insinuates that the way we receive the Spirit is no different from the way we receive Christ's gift of forgiveness and salvation—by faith.

Before the Galatians have enough time to ponder this, Paul hits them with a second question: "How foolish can you be? After starting your Christian lives in the Spirit, why are you now trying to become perfect by your own human effort? Have you experienced so much for nothing? Surely it was not in vain, was it?" (Gal 3:3–4). Reiterating his assertion on the foolishness of the Galatians, Paul shows them the inconsistency of their thinking by explaining that the way we begin the Christian life is the same way we continue living as a Christian. Initially, we must take a step of faith, but progressively, we must continue to walk in faith. To begin by faith and then try to continue by legalism is to nullify the effect of the gospel.

The post-conversion experience is referred to as "trying to become perfect." Paul is not talking about moral perfection, for this is not achievable by human effort, but rather spiritual maturity (as the word "perfect" is often used in Pauline literature). It is an allusion to a believer's growth and maturity after the initial act of receiving the gospel by faith. The false teachers had insisted that while faith is needed to kick-start the redemptive process, believers must adhere to Jewish laws in addition to believing in the Lord Jesus Christ. Paul adamantly disagrees with this and even says that such a requirement diminishes the beauty of grace-based conversion to virtually nothing—it is all in vain. The way Paul makes this assertion leaves little room for the Galatians to disagree, thereby forcing them to acknowledge that the gospel of Christ was fully sufficient for salvation and spiritual growth.

Paul's final question is a repetition of the first. He writes, "I ask you again, does God give you the Holy Spirit and work miracles among you because you obey the law? Of course not! It is because you believe the message you heard about Christ" (Gal 3:5). The repetition, however, comes with a twist. Whereas Paul's first question focuses on receiving the Spirit, this one focuses on God giving the Spirit. Although Paul is clearly talking about two sides of the same coin, the shift from receiver to giver is significant because it reminds us that any human attempt to become righteous pales in the light of God's power to make us righteous by his own will and power. So powerful is the gift of the Holy Spirit that it manifests itself in the form of miracles. A miracle is an absurdity in that it violates human logic and the laws of natural physics. It is a supernatural phenomenon that finds no explanation in the natural world. Thus, it cannot be a product of human effort. That they actually have experienced such miracles proves Paul's point all the more. If they have believed the message of Christ by faith, why would they even try to compete with God, who is clearly more powerful and gracious than they? Very foolish indeed!

Case in Point

After stunning the Galatians with a barrage of rapid-fire inquiries, Paul pauses to give them a chance to process his questions. Earlier, he had talked about how his readers had a clear picture of what was accomplished by the death of Christ. Here, he paints another picture to illustrate the concept of justification by faith. He writes, "In the same way, 'Abraham believed God, and God counted him as righteous because of his faith'" (Gal 3:6). Amazingly, he does not use a contemporary illustration to clarify his point. Instead, he reaches back into history and brings up an old but familiar story. There are some who mistakenly assume that the Old Testament is characterized by the law, while the New Testament is characterized by grace. Paul, however, wants us to understand that the grace of God has always been at work, undergirding his redemptive plan throughout all the ages. What better way to demonstrate this point than to revisit the story of Abraham's own redemption?

The reference to Abraham's story is especially fitting because it addresses the Judaizers' claim that those who are under the law have an advantage over those who are not. The false teachers were particularly proud of belonging to the lineage of Abraham and insinuated that their bloodline gave them a special blessing that Gentiles did not share. While there are indeed many things that made Jews unique, having exclusive claim to God's grace was not one of them. This work of grace is made available to all, whether or not they are direct descendants of Father Abraham. Furthermore, the Judaizers may have forgotten that like most of the Galatian readers, Abraham was originally a pagan. It is in this sense that the Galatian Gentiles are able to relate to his story.

Abraham, whose original name was Abram, came from Ur of the Chaldeans, a land that is better known today as the greater Iraqi area. Later, he and his family settled in the village of Haran (Gen 11:31). The Bible tells us he was a wealthy man, and according to Hebrew historians, his father was an idol maker and worshipper. It is curious, therefore, that God would choose such an unlikely individual to be the father of a new nation—a nation whose primary identity was that of *God's chosen people*. The call of Abraham represents a radical shift in the redemptive plan of God and also reveals how gracious and loving he truly is.

On a day Abraham would never forget, the Lord said to him,

> Leave your native country, your relatives, and your father's family, and go to the land that I will show you. I will make you into a great nation. I will bless you and make you famous, and you will be a blessing to others. I will bless those who bless you and curse those who treat you with contempt. All the families on earth will be blessed through you. (Gen 12:1–3)

With these words, God initiated a covenant relationship with Abraham. Remarkably, the focus of this covenant is on the promises of God, which suggests that the efficacy of the agreement primarily rests in God's willingness and ability to hold up his part of the deal. We see this in four crucial statements, prefaced by "I will." The Lord said, "I will show you" (a land), "I will make you a great nation," "I will bless you and make you famous," and "I will bless those who bless you." And because God is always true to his promises, this covenant with Abraham secured his status as one who was chosen and blessed.

Each believer is a chosen individual, and Abraham is our prototype. The elements of his call—from God's initiation of the relationship to the giving of the covenant and the pronouncement of blessings—are found in our own salvific experiences, even though the circumstances surrounding our experience is different each time. And, as Paul points out, the most significant aspect of chosenness is that the condition by which one is justified has always remained the same; that is, we are all justified *by faith*. Abraham's faith is highlighted by the author of Hebrews who wrote, "It was by faith that Abraham obeyed when God called him to leave home and go to another land that God would give him as his inheritance. He went without knowing where he was going" (Heb 11:8).

The covenant between God and Abraham was sealed with the sign of circumcision, which involved the removal of the foreskin of a male's sexual organ. This sign was to be upon Abraham and all his children. Until this very day, people of Jewish origin continue to practice circumcision in obedience to this ancient covenant. However, there were some who mistakenly assumed that Abraham was justified by his work of obedience (e.g., being circumcised) rather than by faith. But this is putting the cart before the horse. We must never confuse a sign with that which it symbolizes. In this case, circumcision was but a sign of a greater reality that validated Abraham's justification. That is, he was justified because he believed. And because he believed, God gave him and his descendants a sign by which they would be able to distinguish themselves from those who are not part of the covenant.

Paul makes it clear to his readers that we share Abraham's inheritance not on the basis of circumcision but on the basis of faith. He said, "The real children of Abraham, then, are those who put their faith in God" (Gal 3:7). The apostle connects the past with the present by asserting that just as Abraham was counted righteous because of faith, so are those who have faith in God's promises today. So who is the real child of Abraham? Not someone who is simply Jewish by birth and circumcised according to the law but rather one who is justified by faith in the redemptive work of Jesus Christ.

The Judaizers in Galatia must have certainly received this point loud and clear. After all, they would have taken much pride in their direct lineage from Abraham and their continued practice of circumcision. Imagine their shock when Paul declares that neither Abrahamic lineage nor circumcision provided any merit with regards to receiving the blessing of Christ's gift of salvation. This was a definite blow to the false teachings being proliferated among the churches in Galatia. Paul is very clear about this: there are not two ways to righteousness; there is only one way. Faith in Christ is the only requirement to receive the full blessing of salvation.

Then, turning his attention to the Gentile readers in Galatia, Paul writes,

> What's more, the Scriptures looked forward to this time when God would declare the Gentiles to be righteous because of their faith. God proclaimed this good news to Abraham long ago when he

said, "All nations will be blessed through you." So all who put their faith in Christ share the same blessing Abraham received because of his faith. (Gal 3:8–9)

Paul reminds his readers that the salvation of Gentiles was not an addendum to God's original plan. Instead, God had always intended non-Jews to be included in his cosmic plan of redemption. It is also important to note that this declaration was given long before the law was given to Moses. Therefore, a plan of salvation based on grace rather than the law has been the standard of God's redemptive plan from the very beginning. In light of this revelation, the Judaizers' claim that salvation must include adherence to the Mosaic law was ultimately pointless. Let me once again clarify that this is not to say the law had no purpose but instead that the purpose of the law was primarily to expose the need for salvation rather than to be the source of it.

One of the highlights of the doctrine of justification by faith is that it supersedes the issue of race. Faith is something anyone can exercise, regardless of ethnic origin. This is why God could have declared confidently to Abraham that even the Gentiles would be declared righteous, because they are just as capable of believing as any Jewish person would be. For this reason, the blessing of the Gentile believer is essentially no different from that of one who is a direct descendant of Abraham.

The Inefficacy of the Law

What do we make of those who insist on pursuing righteousness by obeying the law? Is this not, after all, a noble task? Perhaps it is. But the question Paul is addressing is not nobility but efficacy. It is not a matter of how gallant the pursuit of righteousness is but rather how effective the pursuit is in attaining a right standing with God. It is in this sense that the teachings of the Judaizers are fundamentally flawed.

Furthermore, Paul exposes the impotence of the law with regards to redemption when he wrote, "But those who depend on the law to make them right with God are under his curse, for the Scriptures say, 'Cursed is everyone who does not observe and obey all the commands that are written in God's Book of the Law'" (Gal 3:10). Having just argued for the merits of justification by faith, he now offers the flipside of the same argument. This manner of reasoning via contrast was a common form of argumentation in Paul's day. Assuming any of his readers would insist on depending on the law for justification, Paul reminds them that this path would actually lead to a curse. What a contrast to the blessing believers would otherwise receive if the path of faith were followed! The distinction could not be any clearer.

In what way would observing the law be a curse? Paul addresses this question by quoting from Deut 27. In this Old Testament passage, Moses charges God's people to follow the will of God and presents them with a series of blessings and curses as an incentive for obedience. Moses ends by saying, "Cursed is anyone who does not affirm and obey the terms of these instructions" (Deut 27:26). In Paul's rendition of this passage, he presents an all-or-nothing approach to following the law. That is, one must obey all of the law or not obey at all. And who is able to perfectly obey all of the law? No one, of course. Anyone who wants to be made righteous by obeying the law is doomed to fail from the onset and is, therefore, cursed. The law is a harsh taskmaster because it demands nothing less than perfect compliance, and failure to do so results in condemnation regardless of how severe or negligible the transgression might be.

This concept of sin is carried over even in the New Testament. The Greek word for sin (*hamartia*) literally means "to miss the mark." It illustrates a failure to hit an intended target. In this case, it is a failure to measure up to the splendor of God's holiness. In his letter to the Romans, Paul declared, "For everyone has sinned; we all fall short of God's glorious standard" (Rom 3:23). Suppose two men are trapped by the ledge of a mountain and attempt to jump to another ledge ten feet away. The first man jumps but misses by five feet. The second man jumps but misses by only two feet. It doesn't make any difference by how far each man missed his mark, for to miss by any distance short of ten feet means that they both fall to their death.

Likewise, anyone who attempts to fulfill the whole law yet misses by any measure is cursed to suffer the consequence of sin, which is ultimately spiritual death, or eternal separation from God. This is why Paul contends,

> So it is clear that no one can be made right with God by trying to keep the law. For the Scriptures say, "It is through faith that a righteous person has life." This way of faith is very different from the way of law, which says, "It is through obeying the law that a person has life." (Gal 3:11–12)

Paul has full clarity on this issue and expects the Galatians to likewise see his point for what it is. The law has no power to save. Paul again quotes from an Old Testament passage to affirm that the righteous will live by faith

(Hab 2:4). The use of this passage is an intentional attempt to show the Galatians—and the false teachers among them—that even in the Hebrew Scriptures, faith has always been God's prescribed path to righteousness.

In verse twelve, Paul alludes to Lev 18:5, which says, "If you obey my decrees and my regulations, you will find life through them." It is conceivable that this passage was being used by the Judaizers to back up their position. Yet Paul uses it to contrast the way of faith with the way of the law. Once again, Paul is not denying that obeying the law is important (or noble); however, he makes it clear that because no one is able to fully live up to the demands of the law, the way of faith is ultimately the sinner's only hope for salvation. The way of the law and the way of faith are simply diametrically opposed and, therefore, unacceptable as dual means of obtaining the righteousness of God.

Christ the Curse-Breaker

If a person is pursuing the path of the law, how can he or she be released from the impending curse that results from this false pursuit? The answer is found in the person and work of Jesus Christ. As if he were appealing to those in Galatia who were still unconvinced of his previous assertions, Paul writes,

> But Christ has rescued us from the curse pronounced by the law. When he was hung on the cross, he took upon himself the curse for our wrongdoing. For it is written in the Scriptures, "Cursed is everyone who is hung on a tree." Through Christ Jesus, God has blessed the Gentiles with the same blessing he promised to Abraham, so that we who are believers might receive the promised Holy Spirit through faith. (Gal 3:13–14)

Because people are sinners who are hopelessly depraved, we are all in desperate need of a Savior. It is interesting that Paul had waited only until now to mention the name of Christ. It's as if he wanted the reader to feel a deep sense of despondency, leaving us longing for someone to rescue us from our cursed state. And Jesus Christ alone is that rescuer we all seek. It is in this sense that the gospel is truly *good news*.

Paul begins with the phrase "but Christ." There could be no simpler, yet more powerful words than these. They speak of God's power to undo all that the curse had done. No matter how dire the human condition is under the law, the power of Christ is able to liberate us from it to experience eternal life, which we were always meant to enjoy.

When Paul says that Christ rescued us, he used a term that literally means "to purchase out of slavery." Our spiritual enslavement comes to an end when we meet Christ at his cross. And how exactly did Christ secure our redemption? By taking the curse of our sins upon himself as he hung on Calvary's cross. To illustrate his point, Paul makes a fascinating reference to a regulation stipulated in the Old Testament. In the book of Deuteronomy, Moses wrote, "If someone has committed a crime worthy of death and is executed and then hanged on a tree, the body must never remain on the tree overnight. You must bury the body that same day, for anyone hanging on a tree is cursed of God" (Deut 21:22–23). It is interesting that the cross of Christ is often referred to as a "tree." How fitting then to see that the curse that should have been placed on us was instead put upon Christ so that we might be set free from its consequences. If we respond to God by faith, we are no longer slaves to sin and its curse but are now free to live the rest of our lives for his glory.

True to his previous point, Paul once again stresses that the lifting of the curse is not a limited blessing only for Jews but is made available to Gentiles as well. Because both Jews and Gentiles are capable of believing in Christ, they are equally qualified to be released from the curse of sin and blessed with the promise of the Holy Spirit. This gift is not contingent on adherence to the law but on the grace received by faith.

What, then, do we make of the law now that we know it has no power to save? Perhaps these words by the author of Hebrews can shed some light on the matter,

> The old system in the law of Moses was only a shadow of the things to come, not the reality of the good things Christ has done for us. The sacrifices under the old system were repeated again and again, year after year, but they were never able to provide perfect cleansing for those who came to worship. If they could have provided perfect cleansing, the sacrifices would have stopped, for the worshipers would have been purified once for all time, and their feelings of guilt would have disappeared. (Heb 10:1–2)

So here we see that the purpose of the law was to give us a glimpse of things to come. It was as a shadow that resembled the fullness of God's redemptive blessing, but it was not the blessing itself. It would be foolish to be enamored with a person's shadow while completely ignoring the person himself. Likewise, a fascination with the law at the expense of Christ is equally foolish. It is little wonder, then, that Paul marveled at the Galatians' folly. With the help of God's Word and his Spirit, may we all be spared from such lunacy and wisely follow the path of grace through faith.

6

A Promise Is a Promise

Galatians 3:15–22

WE DO IT ALL the time. Make promises, that is. A witness swears to tell the truth, a kid crosses her heart, a person with addictive behavior writes down his New Year's resolution, a politician guarantees reform, and a husband swears on his mother's grave. But too often we take such pledges so lightly that we don't think twice about rescinding on our promises. You know how it works—the witness lies under oath, the kid crosses her fingers while crossing her heart, the addict rolls weed in the very paper he wrote the resolution on, the politician folds under pressure, and mothers all around the world are rolling in their graves.

Every now and then, however, we hear a story that renews our confidence in the practice of making a promise. Take the case of Kathy Strong. In 1972, Kathy was given a trinket known as a MIA-POW bracelet. Each was engraved with the name of an American serviceman imprisoned in Vietnam. The point of the bracelet was to make sure that the American people did not forget these prisoners. Kathy's bracelet had the name of James Leslie Moreland, an elite Army Green Beret. She cherished this gift, vowing to keep the bracelet on until Moreland returned home, not knowing that this would not happen for another thirty-eight years. Amazingly, she even kept the bracelet on during an MRI scan. The technicians just had to make sure her arm was not in the machine. In 2011, the remains of James Moreland were discovered and identified, then eventually brought home to be buried. On the day of the burial, Kathy Strong slipped the bracelet off her hand and placed it on the sleeve of Moreland's uniform. The promise was made, and the promise was kept.

Two thousand years ago, God fulfilled an even more impressive promise. Through the sacrificial death of Christ, He completed the terms of his redemptive covenant with us, thereby rendering powerless all other means of attaining righteousness. In his letter to the Galatians, Paul continues to drive home this very important point.

A Promise Is a Promise

In the previous chapter, we discussed the inefficacy of the law. Here, we will contrast the law with the promise and reveal the efficacy, and therefore the superiority, of God's promise. In true diatribe fashion, Paul takes on the posture of an apologist who is prepared to argue in favor of the very assertions he set forth earlier in his letter. Furthermore, he will expound on the role of God's promise while clarifying its relationship with the law.

Good apologists are like good chess players. In the same way a grandmaster anticipates the future moves of his opponent, Paul anticipates how his readers are going to respond to his epistle. He is fully cognizant that some of the Galatian readers remain unconvinced by his arguments against the limitations of the law. He also presumes some of the objections they will raise as they read his letter. Specifically, Paul appears to anticipate four objections.

First, the Galatians might argue that the law can be amended to accommodate the way of grace. Second, they might question the veracity of Paul's teaching and accuse him of inventing a new doctrine. Third, they might sarcastically argue that since salvation is by grace, then the law must certainly be useless. And fourth, they might assert that not only is the law useless, it may very well be utterly evil in that it lies in opposition to the message of grace.

Galatians 3:15–22 contains Paul's response to these anticipated objections.

The Law Is a Binding Agreement

Paul wrote to the Galatians, "Dear brothers and sisters, here's an example from everyday life. Just as no one can set aside or amend an irrevocable agreement, so it is in this case" (Gal 3:15). Although Paul is continuing the argument he started in the first part of the third chapter, it is worth noting that Paul is taking a different approach this time around. He began the third chapter by referring to his readers as "foolish Galatians" (Gal 3:1), but now he calls them "dear brothers and sisters" (Gal 3:15). What a contrast! The former is a term of reprimand, but the latter is a term of endearment. Could it be that after getting their attention with such forthright candor, Paul is now inviting his readers to reason with him as members of God's family? What a fitting reminder that even though believers sometimes experience conflict, the bond we have in Christ is strong enough to keep us united.

The apostle points out that the law is a legally binding agreement that is not subject to alterations. That is why the false teachers are in error when they insist that salvation is a product of obeying the law *plus* believing in Christ. Such a formulation would require amending the demands of the law by adding a stipulation that was not originally agreed upon. This would simply be unacceptable.

To drive his point home, Paul used an illustration from the ancient practice of covenant-agreement. He notes that his example is taken from everyday life. The term "everyday life" must be understood in light of its historical context. What he is about to say may not necessarily be true today, but it was certainly true at the time he wrote these words. In Paul's day, legal agreements were not subject to amendments or alterations. In Greek law, such agreements were registered in the office of municipal records. Once recorded, even the parties that originally formed such agreements could not change these documents. Likewise, the law of God is something that is set in stone (both literally and figuratively) and cannot be tampered with.

The term "agreement" comes from the Greek term *diatheke* and is rendered as "covenant" in other English translations of the Bible. It literally means "a disposition of property by will." The modern use of the term "covenant" implies an agreement between two or more parties that is governed by a bilateral commitment to fulfill the terms agreed upon. Interestingly, this is not necessarily the case with the ancient use of the term. In the Bible, a covenant can actually be based on a unilateral agreement wherein only one party is expected to fulfill the terms of the agreement.

We see a great example of this in Gen 15. The Abrahamic covenant was an agreement between God and Abraham wherein the Lord promised to bless Abraham with a child and, subsequently, make him the father of a great nation that would make the promised land their dwelling. The fifteenth chapter of Genesis narrates how this covenant was ratified. After God promised to give Abraham the land, he asked the Lord, "How can I be sure that I will actually possess it?" In response, God instructed him to take a young cow, a goat, a ram, a turtledove, and a pigeon. Abraham then took the animals (except the birds) and cut them in half, laying each half on the ground with a path open down the middle. Interestingly, the verb form of the word covenant means "to cut or divide." Normally at this point, the two agreeing parties would then walk between the divided carcasses while spelling out the stipulations of their agreement. In the end, they would proclaim that should anyone fail to fulfill their end of the deal, that person would be cursed to share the same fate as that of the animals on the ground.

Amazingly, this is not what happened in the story. Instead of God and Abraham walking between the carcasses, the Bible says,

> After the sun went down and darkness fell, Abram [Abraham's pre-covenant name] saw a smoking firepot and a flaming torch pass between the halves of the carcasses. So the Lord made a covenant with Abram that day and said, "I have given this land to your descendants, all the way from the border of Egypt to the great Euphrates River." (Gen 15:17–18)

As we can see, only God (symbolized by the flaming torch) walked between the carcasses while Abraham witnessed this as a mere spectator. From this, we can surmise that the covenant was not bilateral, but instead was unilateral. That is, the agreement rested on the faithfulness of God alone, independent of Abraham's involvement.

Do you understand why we shouldn't confuse religiosity with righteousness? Religiosity is an attempt to *partner* with God in hopes of attaining a state of holiness. Biblical righteousness, on the other hand, is a gift that God bestows upon us solely on the basis of what Jesus did for us at Calvary's cross. Jesus died for us in order to satisfy the terms of this new covenant. Our part is to simply receive his gift with thanksgiving, submission, and lifelong gratitude.

Paul went on to write, "God gave the promise to Abraham and his child. And notice that the Scripture doesn't say 'to his children,' as if it meant many descendants. Rather, it says, 'to his child'—and that, of course, means Christ" (Gal 3:16). Rather than amend the old covenant, God established a new covenant—one that was based on a promise, not a law. The promise, of course, finds it fulfillment in the person of Jesus Christ.

In this verse, Paul employs a typical rabbinic method of discourse involving wordplay. He points to the particular use of the term "child" as opposed to "children" (the original text actually renders it "seed" versus "seeds"). Some scholars argue that this verse is problematic because in English, both "seed" and "seeds" can carry connotations of plurality. This clearly does not sidetrack Paul, as he simply wants to draw attention to the obvious emphasis implied by the term "child."

There is an allusion here to the original Messianic promise given in Gen 3:15, where God said to the tempter,

> And I will cause hostility between you and the woman,
> and between your offspring and her offspring [i.e., "seed"].
> He will strike your head, and you will strike his heel.

Although it would not have been obvious to the original readers of Genesis, we who read the Bible in hindsight postulate that the woman's "seed" is a reference to the Messiah, Christ Jesus himself. And in the letter to the Galatians, Paul clearly affirms this teaching, as he states it in no uncertain terms.

But what exactly is the relationship between Abraham and Jesus? It would appear that Abraham represents all believers, as he is poised as the original heir of God's promise. Christ, on the other hand, has two roles. He is the ultimate heir of what is God's, and he is the one who fulfills the terms of God's promise to us. Roman law permitted covenants to have both an original heir and a subsequent heir. Subsequent heirs are named in a covenant, such as a will, in anticipation of the death of the original heir. The subsequent heir is eligible to receive everything willed to the original heir. So in the case of God's covenant with us, the death of Abraham does not nullify the agreement because Christ is stipulated as the subsequent heir of the promise. He is the recipient of all of God's blessings and favor, and, in his grace, endows the same blessings to those who believe in him. Paul upheld this principle when he wrote to the Romans, "Since we are his children, we are his heirs . . . In fact, together with Christ we are heirs of God's glory" (Rom 8:17).

The Promise Predates the Law

After affirming the binding nature of the law, Paul now shifts his attention to the promise. By this we mean the messianic promise, the vow to send a redeemer to save a lost humanity. This promise was imbedded in the Abrahamic covenant, and so Paul wrote, "This is what I am trying to say: The agreement made with Abraham could not be canceled 430 years later when God gave the law to Moses . . . God would be breaking his promise" (Gal 3:17).

Paul anticipated that the false teachers might accuse him of inventing a new teaching that contradicts the old covenant. Jesus himself was criticized this way many times by religious leaders. Each time, Jesus asserted that he did not intend to contradict the law but rather to fulfill it. In similar fashion, Paul asserts that he has no interest in opposing the law; rather, his intent is to explain the role, function, and results of God's promise.

When he says, "the agreement made with Abraham," Paul is arguing that his teaching regarding God's promise is not new. After all, many centuries had passed since this promise was given to Abraham. Moreover, the fact that the promise was given during the time of Abraham indicates that this agreement predates the giving of the law. Paul even specifies that the former came 430 years prior to the latter.

There is some confusion on the use of "430 years." In Exod 12:40, the number 430 describes how many years the Hebrew people lived in Egypt. However, in the Septuagint (the Greek translation of the Hebrew Scriptures, often rendered LXX in honor of the seventy scholars who were involved in producing this translation), 430 describes the number of years between the time of Abraham and the time of Moses. It is apparent that Paul bases his comment on the information found in the LXX. Bottom line: the emphasis of the text is not on the historical content but on the historical sequence.

In any case, Paul's point remains intact—that the promise came even before there was such as thing as the Mosaic law. Furthermore, this promise was not nullified when the law was given, since it clearly remained in effect from the time it was given. During the period of the prophets, the emphasis continued to be on God's promises rather than on the law. For instance, the prophet Jeremiah wrote,

> "The day is coming," says the Lord, "when I will make a new covenant with the people of Israel and Judah. This covenant will not be like the one I made with their ancestors when I took them by the hand and brought them out of the land of Egypt. They broke that covenant, though I loved them as a husband loves his wife," says the Lord. "But this is the new covenant I will make with the people of Israel on that day," says the Lord. "I will put my instructions deep within them, and I will write them on their hearts. I will be their God, and they will be my people. And they will not need to teach their neighbors, nor will they need to teach their relatives, saying, 'You should know the Lord.' For everyone, from the least to the greatest, will know me already," says the Lord. "And I will forgive their wickedness, and I will never again remember their sins." (Jer 31:31–34)

This promise, given to Abraham and cherished by all God's people, is sure and unchanging. It cannot be cancelled by anyone; otherwise God would be a promise-breaker, which he is not. And because of this, you and I have every reason to continue holding on to this promise and enjoying all its benefits through Christ Jesus.

To remove all doubt, Paul pushes his argument further and writes, "For if the inheritance could be received by keeping the law, then it would not be the result of accepting God's promise . . . But God graciously gave it to Abraham as a promise" (Gal 3:18). The apostle is giving us a reasonable and objective foundation for accepting God's promise. Simply put, if obeying that law was the only requirement for salvation, why would God bother making a promise? It just doesn't make sense.

Fulfilling the law requires works. But we are not saved by works. Instead, we are saved by grace through faith (Eph 2:8–9). The doctrine of salvation by grace is clearly not new, as some of the Galatian readers might have supposed, for many centuries ago, Abraham himself was saved by God's gracious favor. God gave righteousness as a gift to Abraham. All Abraham had to do was receive it by faith. This precious gift is not only given to Abraham; it is given to you as well. As the beloved Scripture says, "For God loved the world so much that he gave his one and only Son, so that everyone who believes in him will not perish but have eternal life" (John 3:16).

The law and the promise lay on opposite sides of a spectrum and are not to be confused with each other. They are each given for a specific purpose, and, as such, they are each designed to produce a specific result. Knowing this difference is key to understanding what Paul is asserting in this epistle.

The Law Has a Shelf Life

Since the law cannot accomplish the same thing as the promise, does it mean the law is useless? Of course not. Paul is not anti-law; he simply wants the Galatians to understand the rightful place of the law in God's redemptive plan. He writes, "Why, then, was the law given? It was given alongside the promise to show people their sins. But the law was designed to last only until the coming of the child who was promised. God gave his law through angels to Moses, who was the mediator between God and the people" (Gal 3:19).

The law serves an important role for all of humanity. Without the law, we would not be aware of our sins. Consequently, we would not seek to be freed from sin and its consequences. The law does not make us righteous, but it is necessary to reveal our need for righteousness.

Think of the law as a mirror. A mirror helps us see a reflection of ourselves. Isn't it amazing that we have never truly seen ourselves? Others have seen us, but we never have. The best we can do is to see our likeness in a mirror. So imagine you have a smudge on your forehead. You are totally oblivious that it is there. Then you chance upon a mirror, and there you see the smudge. The mirror has successfully shown you what is on your forehead, and it almost seems to ask you to do something about it. The mirror, however, has one major limitation—it can reveal that you are dirty, but it cannot do anything to make you clean. For that, you need something else, like soap and water.

The law functions in much the same way as the mirror. It does a great job exposing our sins and revealing things about our lives that need to be changed. Yet that very same law has neither the power to change us, nor to make us clean. For that, we need the redemptive grace of God. And this grace comes through the promised Messiah, our Lord Jesus Christ. Do you now see how Paul can accurately say that the law was "given alongside the promise to show people their sins"?

Furthermore, once the law has accomplished its intended purpose, it soon outlives its usefulness. Hence, it has a definite shelf life. That is not to say that the law was never needed, but it must not be counted on beyond its intended function. The problem is, some laws are not routinely examined to find out whether they are still relevant or necessary. Consider, for instance, these California laws (some of which are still officially in effect):

- It is a misdemeanor to shoot any kind of game from a moving vehicle, unless the target is a whale.
- No vehicle without a driver may exceed sixty miles per hour.
- Peacocks have the right of way to cross any street, including driveways.
- It is illegal to ride a bicycle in a swimming pool.
- Citizens are not permitted to wear cowboy boots unless they already own at least two cows.
- Detonating a nuclear device within the city limits results in a $500 fine.[1]

1. "Dumb Laws in California," *The Dumb Network*, 2016, www.dumblaws.com/laws/

Silly, aren't they? Yet there was a time when each of these laws was deemed necessary given the unique situation under which it was passed. Yet as times change or as a rule ceases to be relevant, it is necessary to acknowledge that such laws no longer have any authoritative power over citizens. In the case of the old covenant, Paul said that "the law was designed to last only until the coming of the child who was promised," an obvious reference to Jesus Christ. The law's function was to point to our need for a rescuer. Jesus Christ himself came as that Rescuer. Consequently, we are saved by Christ, not by the law.

There is an interesting footnote in Gal 3:19, where Paul says the law was given "through angels to Moses." Some Jews held the belief that the law of Moses was delivered by angels—a conjecture based on a loose interpretation of Deut 33:2 and Ps 68:17. That Paul makes reference to this suggests he agreed with this belief. In any case, it was beyond doubt that Moses was a mediator between God and his people.

Paul points out that the need for a mediator is another distinction between the law and the promise. He wrote, "Now a mediator is helpful if more than one party must reach an agreement. But God, who is one, did not use a mediator when he gave his promise to Abraham" (Gal 3:20). Once again, Paul maintains that the law was a bilateral agreement, whereas the promise was a unilateral one. The former was an agreement between two parties, while the promise was a one-sided vow to bless Abraham and his people.

In his letter to Timothy, Paul talks about another mediator when he writes, "For there is only one God and one Mediator who can reconcile God and humanity—the man Christ Jesus. He gave his life to purchase freedom for everyone" (1 Tim 2:5–6). Moses was an able mediator who faithfully represented God before the people and the people before God. Christ, however, is a superior mediator because he is not only a representative, but also a Savior who, through his sacrifice, reconciles people to God once and for all time. He alone has the right to claim, "I am the way, the truth, and the life . . . No one can come to the Father except through me" (John 14:6).

The Law and the Promise Are Friends

Finally, Paul addresses the last of the four anticipated objections his readers might raise; that is, "Is the law evil, since it lies opposite the promise?" To

---

united-states/california.

this, Paul responds, "Is there a conflict, then, between God's law and God's promises? Absolutely not! If the law could give us new life, we could be made right with God by obeying it" (Gal 3:21). Just because two things are opposite does not mean they are opposed to each other. On the contrary, opposites often tend to complement each other. This is the case between the law and the promise. Paul is emphatic in rejecting the idea that they are in conflict with each other.

In more ways than one, my wife and I are opposites. I am an introvert, while Ana is an extrovert; I am perpetually clueless, while she is deeply intuitive; I think the Three Stooges were comedic geniuses, whereas she prefers the dry wit of British humour (Did you notice how I spelled that?); my idea of a vacation is staying home, but hers is seeking the next great adventure; I crave salt, and she craves sugar; I view shopping as punishment, but she views it as a reward. From what I just described, you would think she and I would not get along, yet we do! We thoroughly enjoy each other's company, we constantly amuse each other, we make great partners in ministry, we parent our children with a great deal of balance, and neither of us can imagine enjoying life without the other. To borrow a phrase from evangelist Billy Graham and his wife, Ruth, Ana and I are "happily incompatible."

In much the same way, Paul helps us realize that the law and the promise are not enemies but friends. Both are given by God, and both serve his greater purpose for humankind. We need to know, however, that righteousness does not come from following the law, for if it did, there would have been no reason for Christ to die on the cross. In fact, the crucifixion of Christ would have been history's greatest folly had there been some other acceptable means of salvation. Obeying the law results in compliance but not completeness. Only Christ, who perfectly satisfied the demands of the law, can do that for us.

Paul ends this section with the assurance "But the Scriptures declare that we are all prisoners of sin, so we received God's promise of freedom only by believing in Jesus Christ" (Gal 3:22). Interestingly, the Apostle Paul does not have to make an argument for human depravity. He merely assumed its veracity based on the biblical claim. In turn, Paul expects that same assumption of his readers.

The belief in the corruption of human nature is often misunderstood in modern culture. Many today assume that people are essentially good and that some are sadly led astray. Yet the biblical worldview posits that because we are a fallen humanity, each person is born with a sinful nature and begins life in the condition of spiritual imprisonment. Our depravity manifests itself in countless ways, including hatred, jealousy, war, sexual perversion, crime, and various forms of disruptive behavior. We are so corrupt that even if we wanted to set ourselves free, we have no capacity to do so. Someone once likened it to a bird with damaged wings. Although it was born with the propensity for flight, it cannot actually fly because of its broken condition.

The sinner's freedom does not come from doing but from believing. The sinner's hope, therefore, is to put faith in a savior other than him or herself—one who is perfect in every way, compassionate toward us, sympathetic to our needs, and gracious enough to bear the sins of the world. Search the pages of history, and you will find only one person who fits the bill. God gave us his living Word, Jesus Christ, who came to make us righteous—just as he promised.

7

Free at Last!

Galatians 3:23–4:7

On August 28, 1963, one of the most memorable speeches in modern history was delivered below the steps of the Lincoln Memorial in Washington, DC. The man responsible for the speech was the Rev. Dr. Martin Luther King Jr., and he told the world about his dream. Among other things, he dreamt that a day would come when his children would "one day live in a nation where they will not be judged by the color of their skin but by the content of their character."[1] In a time of great civil unrest when skin color divided a nation, Dr. King captured the hearts and minds of people everywhere. His words were so masterfully spoken that they have yet to find a rival as far as many are concerned.

Every year, the third Monday of January is set aside to commemorate the day of Dr. King's birth. Each year, I've made it a habit to reflect on his famous speech. As I relive the moment, I am struck by his eloquence, his candor, his courage, his conviction, and his ability to cast a vision—a picture of a desired future. In this seventeen-minute oration, one man's dream becomes the dream of an entire nation. My favorite part of "I Have a Dream" is the way King ends with the words "Thank God Almighty, we are free at last!"

Anyone who has ever experienced confinement has longed to be set free. I've never been incarcerated, but as a child, I was once stuck in a bathroom. Don't be quick to judge. You'd be surprised to discover how much those two situations have in common. For one thing, there is usually a perfectly good reason for getting in. And once you're in, it doesn't take long for you to want to get out.

My brush with confinement took place when I was about ten years old and our family celebrated Christmas at my aunt's house. No one told

---

1. Martin Luther King Jr., "I Have a Dream" (speech, Lincoln Memorial, August 28, 1963) http://www.thekingcenter.org/archive/document/i-have-dream-1.

me that the bathroom door had a tendency to jam and that the only way to open it was to give it a good thud on the upper corner. So after using the bathroom, I attempted to open the door, but it wouldn't open! I turned the knob every which way, but nothing worked. I pulled with all my might, but no luck. It soon dawned on me that I had only one hope for freedom—I had to scream like a girl (with all due respect to my female readers). So after screaming for what seemed like an eternity, my aunt and cousins came to my rescue, and soon I was out of harm's way. Not to make light of Dr. King's dream, but all I could think of that time was "Free at last! Free at last! Thank God Almighty, I am free at last!"

Freedom is truly a remarkable gift. Unfortunately, freed people have a tendency to take their liberty for granted. The Galatians had lost sight of the freedom they gained through the work of Christ so completely that they started to entertain the idea that they had yet to be freed and that freedom would come as a result of their religious deeds. Paul is very much concerned about this and clarifies the issue with an uplifting response.

A successful liberation movement involves four elements: knowing the source of oppression, recognizing the most qualified liberator, understanding the process by which freedom is achieved, and appreciating what is attained upon being set free. In Gal 3:23–4:7, Paul addresses all four of these elements.

The Oppression of the Law

Legal guardianship is an ancient concept. Whenever a parent is unavailable to care for a child, whether due to death or temporary absence, another person is given the legal responsibility to watch over that child. Warriors, for instance, assigned such guardians for their children whenever they went off to battle, either to care for the child temporarily until the battle was over or permanently in the event the warrior was killed in action. Resolving the matter of legal child custody is still practiced in virtually every culture today.

Prior to the coming of Christ, the law was given to us to serve as our legal custodian. Paul wrote, "Before the way of faith in Christ was available to us, we were placed under guard by the law . . . We were kept in protective custody, so to speak, until the way of faith was revealed" (Gal 3:23). The image Paul uses is one of a military prison guard who watches over a convict until the time of his trial. The guard is not responsible for the prisoner's freedom, only for his safety. In the same way, the law was given to create a hedge of safety around us, but it was not given to save us.

Human history is marked by many pivotal moments. For Paul, *the* pivotal moment was the time Christ lived among us. Even today, the modern calendar centers on the Christ event. We speak of events taking place before Christ (BC) or since the time of Christ (AD). The coming of Christ ushered in "the way of faith." In the original Greek, the word "faith" is preceded by a definite article. Thus, it is literally translated as "the way of the faith," meaning a specific kind known today as the Christian faith. This faith rests "in Christ," an important distinction when we consider that any faith is only as powerful as its object. If a chair is flimsy, it matters little if I believe strongly that it will hold my weight. No amount of confidence will keep the chair from collapsing once I sit on it. In this case, the object of my faith is weak; therefore, so is my faith. But since Christians put their faith in Christ, this faith is strong because Christ is strong.

However, while Christ had not yet come, God gave us the law to be our guardian. We were kept in its protective custody as it placed a protective hedge around us. The numerous "thou shalt nots" of the law were given to put us in our rightful place and to make us aware of our sins if we went beyond its boundaries. But this role was no longer necessary once the way of faith was revealed. The word "reveal" simply means to make known something that was previously hidden. It speaks to our inability to know without help.

My family and I live by a suburban farm. Each year during harvest season, the farm owners open their property for the public to enjoy the fall harvest. One of the highlights of this event is a gigantic corn maze. Tourists enjoy entering the maze and daring each other to be the first to get out of it. Inevitably, anywhere from three to six people get so lost in the labyrinth that they give up trying. They just don't know how to get out. Fortunately, the farm owners hire aides to help. Because they have an aerial view of the maze, the aides are able to guide the lost souls out of the corn maze. I always enjoy seeing the reactions of those who are finally set free. These people are literally saved as a result of revelation. Someone revealed to them the way out. Likewise, the law, like the corn stalks, provided us with a set of boundaries. Yet it had no ability to reveal to us the way out. Only Christ is able to show us the way to eternal life through faith in him.

To add to his illustration regarding the law, Paul wrote, "Let me put it another way . . . The law was our guardian until Christ came; it protected us until we could be made right with God through faith. And now that the way of faith has come, we no longer need the law as our guardian" (Gal 3:23–25). In the previous verse, Paul likened the law to a custodian; here he likens it to a guardian. In this passage, the word "guardian" is taken from the root word for "pedagogy," the fancy term for the study of being a teacher or instructor. The law, then, is a kind of a teacher. No wonder Paul previously argued that the law is not useless, for it serves an important role in helping us understand more about God and his nature.

By referring to the law as a guardian, Paul affirms that the law is an able tutor. In the ancient world, it was not uncommon for people to hire educated slaves for the sole purpose of tutoring children. Such slaves were highly respected and appreciated because of the influence they had over the child. On the other hand, as they matured, the children likewise developed a great appreciation for their tutors. The tutor remained a slave, but one who was not at all useless.

Laws are a reflection of lawmakers. When I was in college, I had a professor who had this rule: "Never hesitate to ask me questions, for there is no such thing as a stupid question so long as you are willing to learn as a result of discovering the answer." This is not only a great rule, but it is also a useful tool for understanding what kind of teacher he was. With that directive, I learned that my professor was an open-minded sage who wanted me to succeed in my pursuit of learning. God's law does the same.

The rules of God don't save us, but they give us a glimpse of what kind of God he is. The command against adultery shows us he respects fidelity, the command to not bear false witness shows he is a God of truth, and the command to keep the Sabbath shows he values rest and reflection. With each rule, we learn more about him. The law is a good teacher indeed.

As with all good things, even good teaching can come to an end. As King Solomon once said, "For everything there is a season, a time for every activity under heaven . . . A time to search and a time to quit searching" (Eccl 3:1, 6). So it is with the good tutoring we get from the law. Paul said that the law was our teacher "until Christ came." The law successfully taught us about the righteousness of God, but only Christ could actually make us righteous. When a child grows up, that adult no longer needs a tutor, just as when a sinner matures in understanding God's righteousness, that sinner no longer needs the law, for the Spirit who gave the law now dwells in his or her heart.

We've said much about righteousness, but what is it anyway? In his letter to the Galatians, Paul defines righteousness as "being made right with God." It is a legal term from which we get the concept of justification. At the end of a court case, a defendant waits for one of two declarations—guilty or not guilty (notice the use of "not guilty" rather than "innocent," as this terminology is intentional). The declaration, one way or the other, depends on the merits presented during the case. If there was compelling evidence to convict the defendant, then the judgment will be *guilty*. If, however, there is reason to clear the defendant of guilt, the judgment will be *not guilty*. It may very well be that the defendant actually committed the crime, yet there are still circumstances wherein he or she can be exonerated. Such a decision is not reached carelessly, for in order to clear such a person, the decision must be justified. Otherwise, the court will lose credibility, and the judicial system will become nothing more than a farce.

When God justifies a sinner, the decision itself must be justifiable. However, there is a serious problem with the matter of God justifying sinful humanity. One of my early theological mentors, Professor D. C. Barnes, would put it this way: "How can a perfectly just God justify the unjust and remain both Just and Justifier, when in view of divine justice, the unjust have no credentials by which to merit justification?" Sounds simple? It actually is. What Barnes is saying is that God cannot simply justify us on a whim because there is no doubt that we are all guilty of sin (Rom 3:23). If God did, he would cease to be a God of justice.

It's interesting how some people wonder why God can't just forgive humanity with the snap of a finger. No one expects an earthly judge to justify someone without justification, so why do some expect God to do so? We seem to expect more of human judges than we do of God. But God is not only held to a higher standard of justice, he *is* the standard. And yet he justifies us. Why? Because of Jesus! The sacrificial death of Christ on the cross was the perfect and full satisfaction of the demands of God's law. And because of the merits of Christ, all who believe in him as our substitute warrant the declaration of justification—we are not guilty! Now, don't get me wrong. We are undoubtedly guilty for our sinfulness, but in Christ, we are no longer subject to the effects and consequences of sin because we are now righteous in the eyes of God. What a gift! It is surprising that many people still reject it, like some of the Galatians did. They would rather be subject to the tutorial work of the law (which cannot justify us) instead of receiving the free gift of righteousness and eternal life offered to us by God through Christ.

The Liberating Power of Christ

You've heard it said that we are all God's children. This statement, while true in one sense, needs to be qualified. Indeed we are God's children in that each person is a product of his creative power. Paul, however, introduces us to a different dimension of God's parenthood. He wrote, "For you are all children of God through faith in Christ Jesus" (Gal 3:26). The "you" does not refer to all the people of the world. Instead, it refers to those who have faith in Jesus Christ. In his gospel narrative, the Apostle John put it this way: "But to all who believed him and accepted him, he gave the right to become children of God" (John 1:12). Like Paul, John asserts that not every human being is a child of God in the salvific sense. Sonship is a blessing offered to all, but it is a privilege that comes with believing on the Lord Jesus Christ. Even though our physical birth makes us part of the human family, only spiritual birth makes us part of God's family. As John further declared, "They are reborn—not with a physical birth resulting from human passion or plan, but a birth that comes from God" (John 1:13). Jesus will later refer to this as being "born again" (John 3:3).

Being born again is like taking on a new nature. Or as Paul put it, "All who have been united with Christ in baptism have put on Christ, like putting on new clothes" (Gal 3:27). By mentioning baptism, Paul is not teaching that a person becomes a believer upon baptism, as some might believe. In the first century, baptism was an outward symbol of inner change. In other words, you are not a new person because you are baptized; rather, you are baptized as a public affirmation of the inner change that has already taken place in your heart. To be baptized in water without a conversion experience only makes you a wet sinner.

A person who identifies with Christ in baptism is said to be clothed anew. I know of a friend who adopted a teenager. When my friend's adopted daughter was brought home for the first time, she was welcomed with a special jersey embroidered with her new family name. Her new clothes identified her as a member of the family. Those who believe in Jesus become children of God and are spiritually clothed with the righteousness of Christ, which identifies them as members of God's family.

The Judaizers believed they were God's children merely because they were born as Hebrews—direct descendants of their father, Abraham. Moreover, a male Jew born in freedom often felt a great sense of privilege because of his unique status. But with the new covenant in Christ, being a child of God supersedes the quality of ethnicity. It must have come as a surprise when Paul wrote, "There is no longer Jew or Gentile, slave or free, male or female. For you are all one in Christ Jesus. And now that you belong to Christ, you are the true children of Abraham. You are his heirs, and God's promise to Abraham belongs to you" (Gal 3:28–29).

Before we criticize the Judaizers, let me point out that almost everyone in the Greco-Roman world took special pride in their ethnicity, that men were often viewed as superior to women, and that freedom was preferred over slavery. These distinctions created societal barriers that were very difficult, if not impossible, to break. But Christ broke them all! You might object that racial distinctions still exist, that the gender war continues to be fought, and that slavery has not been fully eradicated from the face of the earth. Indeed, all that is true. But what Paul is saying is that in Christ Jesus, these divisions no longer have any power over our ability to be declared righteous through faith and, consequently, be eligible to become children of God. These discriminatory obstacles that so powerfully govern fallen humanity are rendered powerless in the kingdom of God because of the redemptive work of Jesus Christ. By faith, the female Gentile slave could rejoice alongside the male Jewish master because all those societal qualifiers meant nothing in the economy of God. Indeed, all God's spiritual children can be called true children of Abraham, which qualifies them to receive the same blessings promised to the ancient patriarch. For those of us who begin life as wretched sinners, this is a clear testament to the goodness and greatness of God.

The Process of Maturity

Let's approach this issue from a slightly different angle. The liberty we have in Christ is akin to post-juvenile emancipation. In practically every culture throughout human history, adults are held responsible for the care of minor children. Even in cases where a parent dies, another adult is expected to care for such a child. It was no different in Paul's day, as we can very well see when he wrote,

> Think of it this way. If a father dies and leaves an inheritance for his young children, those children are not much better off than slaves until they grow up, even though they actually own everything their father had. They have to obey their guardians until they reach whatever age their father set. (Gal 4:1–2)

There is a fundamental difference between being a child and being a slave. Children are beneficiaries of their parent's inheritance, while slaves are part of that inheritance. Pragmatically, however, they share something in common. In ancient culture, both children and slaves were considered domestic subordinates who were subject to the authority of the head of the household. In fact, Roman law considered the legal status of children and slaves as equal. Even if a child were the apparent heir of a sizable inheritance, he was not free to receive and enjoy that inheritance until he himself became an adult.

Back in 1982, I remember the world rejoicing at the news that a son was born to Prince Charles and his wife Diana. William Arthur Philip Louis, firstborn son of the Prince and Princess of Wales, was a child of destiny. As heir apparent, he is expected to be crowned king of England someday. Yet throughout his childhood, he was a person in custody. Born into royalty yet bound by the authority of his parents, it would be a while before he would reap the fruit of his privileged birth. As William grew up, he was subject to both royal and military training, all in preparation for the future we all knew would be his. It was fascinating to watch him mature into the man he is today. In 2011, we saw a very different William, no longer a child but a young man taking on the role of a husband. Today, he is not merely William, son of Prince Charles, he is now William, Duke of Cambridge. You are I may not be in line for any royal position here on earth, but in the kingdom of God, we are born with the promise of righteousness, which is bestowed upon us when we become spiritually mature.

Those who have not yet experienced Christian liberty are like children who have not yet reached an age of maturity. As spiritual minors, they have the potential to inherit the blessings of God's promise, but in the meantime, they live as slaves to the law and are subject to its harsh rule. That's what religion is—a prison in which one is subject to rules and regulations that are void of a meaningful connection with the God we want to appease. God, on the other hand, does not want us to be religious; he wants us to be righteous. This can only take place once we outgrow our dependence on the law and trust in his grace for forgiveness, salvation, and eternal life.

Each civilization has its own criteria for designating when a child is "grown up." In Judaism, it was around the age of twelve, Greeks set it at eighteen (as it is in modern America), while the Romans left it in the hands of a father to determine what that age would be. Paul had the Roman tradition in mind when he said, "They have to obey their guardians until they reach whatever age their father set" (Gal 4:2).

Paul went on to say, "And that's the way it was with us before Christ came . . . We were like children, we were slaves to the basic spiritual principles of this world" (Gal 4:3). In the original text, the term "spiritual principles" comes from the word for "elements." The modern periodic table contains 118 elements, but people in the ancient world were only aware of four—earth, fire, air, and water. It was not uncommon to ascribe a deity to each one of these elements. In time, these elemental gods were often honored and worshiped as deities that controlled the forces of nature. Soon, polytheistic religions emerged based on the same principle, with a different god for each different facet of life. There was a god who controlled the weather, one who controlled fate, and yet another who controlled the harvest. For the Christian believer, however, these were not gods at all. Far from being a liberating experience, Paul says that subjecting oneself to these false deities was a form of slavery. Only the Lord God can set the human spirit free and lead us to a life of spiritual liberty born out of the righteousness of Christ. To insist on any other path to righteousness would be erroneous at best, and totally wicked at worst, because the consequence of being wrong are deadly and eternal.

The Blessing of Adoption

On the first day of 1863, President Abraham Lincoln issued an executive order known as the Emancipation Proclamation. With the stroke of a pen, 3.1 million slaves were proclaimed freedmen and given the right of American citizenship.[2] For these former slaves, it was a blessing that seemed a long time coming. You see, all slaves dream of freedom, but many get so discouraged with their situation that they succumb to hopelessness. Many African slaves experienced a constant battle between believing slavery would one day be abolished, yet knowing that it might not happen in their lifetime. Imagine the joy of being a slave on the last day of 1862, then waking up

---

2. History.com staff, "Emancipation Proclamation," *History.com*, 2009, http://www.history.com/topics/american-civil-war/emancipation-proclamation.

to freedom the very next day. For 3.1 million people, freedom came at the right time.

About two thousand years ago, Jesus issued an even greater proclamation of freedom—freedom from the tyranny of the law. Paul reminded the Galatians, "But when the right time came, God sent his Son, born of a woman, subject to the law ... God sent him to buy freedom for us who were slaves to the law, so that he could adopt us as his very own children" (Gal 4:4–5). Jesus set us free when the right time came.

The concept of time is an interesting one. There are many words for time in the language used to write the New Testament. Two in particular are noteworthy. First is *chronos*, which means "a space of time" or "the passing of time." Second is *kairos*, which means "in due time" or "the opportune time." Some people refer to it as "the right time." Even in English we acknowledge this distinction, despite the fact that we use the same word. For instance, when we meet a teenage nephew we haven't seen since he was born we might say, "Wow, you've grown so much—how time flies!" We attribute his growth to *chronos*, the passing of time. On the other hand, if you are hanging over a ledge a hundred feet above ground, and just before your hand slips you feel another hand grab yours, you will say to the rescuer, "Wow, you showed up just at the right time!" In this case, you credit the rescuer's heroics to *kairos*, the precise and opportune moment.

The coming of Christ encompasses both *chronos* and *kairos*. In Gal 4:4, Paul reveals this explicitly and implicitly. When he said, "But when the right time came," he actually used the word *chronos*, but he introduced an application of *kairos*. Jesus came in the historical context of the passing of time, and yet he came just at the right time. And what made it the right time? Among other things, Jesus was born during the *Pax Romana*, the period of Roman peace. During this time, the Roman Empire was not engaged in any significant wars. This allowed Joseph and Mary to travel freely between Nazareth and Bethlehem without any fear of danger. Second, the Jewish people were desperate for a Messiah. After years of living under the rule of Gentiles, they longed to be set free by the promised liberator from Yahweh. Even beyond the Jewish context, the world itself needed a savior. Although Rome was not at war, Roman culture was marked by wanton wickedness, not unlike the days of Noah. Even some of the pagans were hoping for meaningful changes to take place in such a society. What a perfect time for Christ to be born. To be certain, he came as the promised

Messiah to the Hebrew people, but he also came to save the world from sin and its consequences.

The coming of Christ refutes the modern philosophy of deism, the belief that although there is a God who created the world, he does not involve himself with the affairs of the world following its creation. Deism posits that God created the world to be self-sufficient and self-sustaining; therefore, God is not necessary for its sustenance. If that were true, then even the problem of sin could have been dealt with through purely naturalistic methods. But we know better, don't we? The Bible is correct in asserting that we sinners cannot set ourselves free. We are utterly in need of a savior, and we find ours in the person of Jesus Christ.

Not only did Jesus come at the right time, he was also "born of a woman," meaning he possessed a human nature. The Bible affirms the doctrine of Christ's dual nature, known as "hypostatic union." That he was sent by God reveals Christ had a divine nature, and that he was born of a woman reveals he had a human nature. He is, as theologians would call him, the "God-man." I may need to address this doctrine in another book someday, but for now, suffice to say that the biblical assertion of who Jesus is remains that he is God in that he is fully divine and also that he is man in that he is fully human. Pragmatically, this addresses the issue presented by the author of Hebrews, who wrote, "Every high priest is a man chosen to represent other people in their dealings with God" (Heb 5:1). Because he now possesses a human nature, Jesus is perfectly qualified to be our High Priest. As the author of Hebrews concluded,

> So then, since we have a great High Priest who has entered heaven, Jesus the Son of God, let us hold firmly to what we believe. This High Priest of ours understands our weaknesses, for he faced all of the same testings we do, yet he did not sin. So let us come boldly to the throne of our gracious God. There we will receive his mercy, and we will find grace to help us when we need it most. (Heb 4:14–16)

As our High Priest, Christ was able to free us from the curse of the law, not by destroying it but by fulfilling it. He was born as one "subject to the law." As you can see, Paul is not out to tear down the law, as the false teachers accused him of doing. Rather, he wants us to understand that we no longer have to be slaves to the law because by fulfilling its demands, Christ has already released us from the law's authority.

How so? The Bible says that the reason God sent Jesus to the world was to "buy freedom" for us. Isn't it ironic that freedom isn't free? In fact, freedom often comes at a great price. Think of people like Mahatma Gandhi, Nelson Mandela, Benazir Bhutto, and Martin Luther King Jr. Each of them paid dearly for the freedom of their people. But none compares with the price Jesus paid for our liberty. In his crucifixion, Christ did not liberate us from mere political powers but from the power of sin and death. As a result, we today are free to enjoy life that is abundant and everlasting.

Furthermore, the death of Christ opens the door for us to become the adopted children of God. After proclaiming that God adopts us as his children, Paul went on to say, "And because we are his children, God has sent the Spirit of his Son into our hearts, prompting us to call out, 'Abba, Father'" (Gal 4:6). Talk about blessing upon blessing! We are not only liberated from the law, we are also adopted into God's family.

Imagine a young delinquent facing a judge in a court of law. Although the young man has been proven to have committed a crime, the judge himself pays the fine for the lad's misdeed, thereby allowing him to be declared not guilty. But instead of sending the boy back to the streets, the judge goes a step further and adopts him as his son. At dawn the man in the black robe was the boy's judge, by midday his redeemer, and by day's end his father. Sounds like the stuff movie dramas are made of, doesn't it? But to those who believe in Christ, this is no feature film; it is instead a true and life-changing experience.

Jesus alone is the only-begotten Son of the Father (John 3:16), but we are still able to become children of God through adoption. The word "adoption" simply means to transfer from one owner to another. Jesus once referred to hypocritical religious leaders as "children of your father the devil" (John 8:44). The righteous, however, have been transformed from children of the devil to children of God.

Growing up in the seventies, adoption was often viewed as taboo. Parents did not openly talk about adopting a child, while adopted children often kept mum about who they were. Thankfully, much has changed. Today, adoption is widely viewed as a wonderful way of being part of a family. In fact, in some ways, it may actually be a little more special. Olympic skater Scott Hamilton was an adopted child and was often teased for it as a young boy. Scott had a great comeback for his tormentors. He would say to them, "My parents chose me, but your parents were stuck with you!" You have to love the guy for having such a keen sense of how special he was, not in spite of being adopted, but because he was adopted.

Greco-Roman laws combined adoption and heirship. This meant that adopted children shared all the rights, responsibilities, and privileges as that of a biological child. In fact, in some countries, it was possible to disown a biological child, but it was illegal to do the same with an adopted child. As adopted children of God, we share in the righteousness and inheritance of Christ. And just as legal adoption required the presence of a witness, the Holy Spirit attests to our divine sonship by blessing us and prompting us to call God "*Abba*, Father." *Abba* is believed to be an Aramaic word used to address a father. But unlike the word Father, which can seem cold or distant, *Abba* is a term of endearment, more akin to "Daddy" or "Pop." We can only call God *Abba* if we have an intimate relationship with him.

As a result of our adoption, Paul told the Galatians, "Now you are no longer a slave but God's own child . . . And since you are his child, God has made you his heir" (Gal 4:7). You see, you can stick to your religiosity and remain a slave to the law. Or you can put your faith in Christ and experience not only liberation from the law, but also the full blessing of being a child of God. With that we can all truly say, thank God Almighty, we are free at last!

8

Losing My Religion

Galatians 4:8–20

BILL AND CINDY COULDN'T wait any longer. Their son, Matt, had been struggling with alcoholism for six years. At first it started with social drinking, but now he was fully hooked. Drinking had led to drugs, and drugs had led to petty theft. These were not merely a series of unfortunate choices. Matt was clearly caught in a lifestyle of addiction. If nothing changed, he was headed for a life in the slammer. Or worse, he would soon end up in the morgue. It was time for an intervention.

An intervention is an attempt to urge a person to seek help in dealing with problem behavior. It becomes especially urgent when the individual has clearly reached the point of losing control over his or her problem. Trapped in a well of their own digging, addicts easily lose perspective of their situation as well as any capacity to rescue themselves. They need a wakeup call, and they need help.

Thankfully, with the love and support of Bill, Cindy, and a carefully selected group of friends, Matt eventually sought the help he needed and is doing much better now.

Addiction can be an awful thing. By "addiction," I mean any habitual participation in an activity or behavior regardless of how harmful that activity or behavior might be. It often begins innocently enough, but soon the addict becomes caught in a trap with no clear path for escape.

There are generally two kinds of addiction. One is substance addiction, which involves getting hooked to things like drugs, alcohol, or nicotine. The other is behavioral addiction, which involves engagement in habitual acts that prove detrimental to the addict's health, be it physically, emotionally, and even socially. This includes addiction to sex, food, unhealthy companionship, and even media (You'd be surprised to learn how many people cannot live without their daily fix of social networking!).

May I suggest that there is another kind of addiction that has plagued humanity for centuries? I'm talking about addiction to religion. Karl Marx once said, "*Die Religion . . . ist das Opium des Volkes,*" meaning "Religion is the opium of the people." You don't have to like Marx to believe his observation holds a grain of truth. An anthropologist once told me that even a casual observation of every known civilization in history reveals that humans are incurably religious. While much of what counts for religious expression can often be harmless, there is a point where religiosity clearly becomes an addiction. For the Apostle Paul, the members of the Galatian church were crossing that threshold into danger.

Addictions can be complicated, and therefore most interventions require the guidance of a professional. However, all interventions generally involve four components. The first step is to help the subject (i.e., addict) understand the gravity of the situation. Second, the subject is urged to change his or her ways by starting on the path to overcoming the addictive substance or behavior. Third, a support structure is built around the subject to guarantee the best chance of overcoming the addiction. And fourth, the subject is asked to take personal responsibility for his or her long-term success.

The Galatians needed an intervention. It was time for them to lose their religion and revert to a healthy biblical understanding of true righteousness. And with what appears to be the precision of a professional therapist, Paul conducts a virtual intervention for his readers.

The Addiction Exposed

Paul begins by exposing the problem. He wrote, "Before you Gentiles knew God, you were slaves to so-called gods that do not even exist" (Gal 4:8). Ironically, the genesis of religious addiction stems from the natural tendency to seek out the Creator of the universe. Unfortunately, this inclination can lead some to false gods and creators. In primitive cultures, people might attribute creative powers to the sun, the wind, or some other cosmic force. The fundamental mistake is to confuse what is with what caused it to be. So in the case of sun worship, people falsely concluded that the sun itself was a god without realizing that the sun was actually made by God. This kind of deficient spirituality led to bondage insofar as people became slaves to these so-called gods. If they knew God for who he really was, they would have been liberated to live in righteousness rather than be imprisoned by their false belief. But because they believed falsely, they became addicted to their religion.

Fooling Ourselves with Fig Leaves

In the 1940s, Lutheran pastor Dietrich Bonhoeffer mourned the religious addiction of the German people. The popularity of Adolf Hitler, accompanied by the rise of the Third Reich, polarized Germany. While some quickly recognized Hitler to be the madman he was, others were mesmerized by his charisma and fully supported his cause. To Bonhoeffer's horror, many religious people were among those who supported Hitler. He was saddened to see how so many churchgoing people remained blindly loyal to their religion even when the religious establishment was leading them away from the truth. In his appeal for sanity, Bonhoeffer called people to embrace what is known today as "religionless Christianity."

At first glance, the term "religionless Christianity" appears to be an oxymoron. But in light of Paul's letter to the Galatians, it makes perfect sense. Without trying to oversimplify a rather complex theological issue, I think Bonhoeffer wanted the German people to distinguish between mere religiosity and biblical righteousness. The former was an addiction that was proving to wreak lethal consequences, while the latter was a gift of God that would lead to a life of freedom and grace.

In much the same way, there remains today a need to differentiate Christendom from Christianity. Christendom is a flawed, human institution marked by traditions that may or may not be biblical at all. Adherence to Christendom can lead to a compliance-based religiosity that is essentially a form of imprisonment. Biblical Christianity, on the other hand, is a form of spirituality that is founded on the teachings of Jesus Christ and harnessed by a loving relationship with God as we are empowered by the Holy Spirit. This relationship with God is made possible through the redemptive work of Jesus Christ on the cross. Not to be confused with Christendom, biblical Christianity liberates the people to be what God always meant for us to be—wonderfully made in his image and likeness and free to exist accordingly (Gen 1:26–27). Having experienced this level of freedom, who would ever think of returning to a life of hopeless imprisonment?

Paul is justified in being appalled by the Galatians who seem to be returning to their former religious life. Note his puzzled tone when he writes, "So now that you know God (or should I say, now that God knows you), why do you want to go back again and become slaves once more to the weak and useless spiritual principles of this world?" (Gal 4:9). This was a rhetorical question in that Paul assumed his readers would also recognize the senselessness of their actions. Their false gods are described as "weak" and "useless" because they have no power to set anyone free from the clutches of sin and death. Could Paul have been any clearer about how he felt? The behavior of the Galatians was simply incomprehensible. Why would anyone taste freedom only to return to a life of imprisonment? Alas, the stronghold of addiction was taking its toll on the Galatians.

To be perfectly honest, I know a thing or two about this irony. Although I've never been medically diagnosed as such, I'm convinced that I have an eating addiction. I realize that most everyone enjoys eating, but as long as I can remember, I've always had a love affair with food, which has resulted in a lifelong struggle with my weight. I jokingly tell people that within the first forty years of my life, I had already lost four hundred pounds! When they give me a puzzled look, I explain that I've lost twenty pounds twenty times. I know something about the frustration of successfully losing twenty pounds of weight, only to go back to my former eating habits, which causes me to regain all the lost weight. Why do I do it? It's an addiction, what else can I say?

The Galatians found themselves in a similar situation. Through Christ, the believers in Galatia had already lost the weight of sin and its consequences, yet here they were returning to their old religious ways. They were going back to a form of religiosity that never gave them true redemption in the first place. Yet they were hooked by their addiction, and Paul was desperate to help them understand that.

This reminds me of the missionary who went to Asia. His host was giving him a tour of the local market when he spotted an elephant next to a fruit stand. He said to his host, "Are we in any danger of that elephant going on a rampage?" "Don't worry," said the host, "the elephant is tied to the ground." To his surprise, the only thing keeping the animal in place was an old rope with one end tied to its leg and the other end tied to a stick planted on the soil. "Surely that is not enough to constrain a beast like that," the missionary said. The host went on to explain why this was not a problem. As it turns out, the moment an elephant like that is born, a chain was tied around its leg with the other end strapped around a mighty tree. All its life, the elephant would try to pull itself free of the chain, but the metal links and the tree would prove too strong. At some point, the elephant concludes that freedom is not possible as long as his leg is bound. Soon, you could fasten anything around the elephant's leg, and this brainwashing ensured it would believe it could never break free. In the end, even an old rope tied to a thin stick was enough to keep it in place.

Somehow, the false teachers in Galatia had so warped the minds of the people that they felt they could not break free from their religious addiction, even though they were already exposed to the gospel message of freedom in Christ. I wonder how many of us find ourselves in the same situation. Christ has already paid the penalty for our sins, yet we live as prisoners of our sinful condition because we refuse to break free of our religious bondage instead of putting our faith in Jesus Christ alone.

Rather than put their faith in Christ, the Galatians were holding on to old religious practices that did not help them gain favor with God. Paul said, "You are trying to earn favor with God by observing certain days or months or seasons or years" (Gal 4:10). Both Paul's Jewish and Gentile readers would be familiar with his reference to observing such holidays. To the Jews, these days, months, and seasons of years would be understood as the Sabbath, recurring celebrations and festivities, and other annual observances such as the year of Jubilee. Gentiles, on the other hand, would be mindful of any number of pagan holidays and festivals that were observed in order to gain favor with the gods. Yet Paul reminded them that observing such feasts, even if they were biblical feasts, could not make them righteous in the eyes of God. If they were to continue such vain practices, Paul mourned, "I fear for you . . . Perhaps all my hard work with you was for nothing" (Gal 4:11).

Perhaps Paul felt like the prophets of old who faithfully proclaimed the messages of God only to see the people ignore the word of the Lord. It must be utterly frustrating to want to help people who don't seem to want to help themselves. In any intervention, it is a pivotal moment when the subject admits his or her need for change. Yet Paul seems unsure whether his readers were prepared to make such a decision. And so his frustration lingered.

The Plea for Change

Paul is indeed frustrated, but he remains mindful that he is writing to God's beloved people. In a rather tender tone he wrote, "Dear brothers and sisters, I plead with you to live as I do in freedom from these things, for I have become like you Gentiles—free from those laws" (Gal 4:12). Paul does not assert his apostolic authority over the Galatians; rather, he appeals to them as a fellow member of the family of God. His concern for them is genuine, and therefore his ultimate goal is not reprimand but restoration.

An intervention must be forceful yet loving. In making a plea for change, the mind and heart are equally involved because while those staging an intervention certainly want their subject to realize the gravity of the situation, they also want him or her to feel that they are on their side. The great Mary Poppins reminded us that "a spoonful of sugar helps the medicine go down, in a most delightful way."[1] Paul would certainly agree.

The nature of Paul's request is a *plea*. This is not a casual request but a strong appeal for change. Religious addiction is a problem of epic proportions, and overcoming this addiction is essential to enjoying the genuine gift of God's righteousness. As it stands, the Galatians were putting up with a cheap imitation of righteousness and were oblivious to the truth that could set them free.

My friend is a coffee aficionado. He is genuinely perturbed to see people drink sub-standard coffee, such as coffee that comes out of vending machines. Every time he sees someone drink a counterfeit cup of joe, he pleads with them to find a good barista who can produce an exquisite brew that will make them forget vending machines ever existed. Some people find my friend snobbish for being so passionate about good coffee. I think he simply knows the real deal and refuses to settle for anything less. In the same way, Paul wants the Galatians to know that it doesn't make sense to put up with a counterfeit spirituality when the gospel has already shown them a better way.

There is also something very personal about Paul's plea. He asked the Galatians to consider living in freedom in the same way he now does. Paul is not asking them to do something he himself has not done. Instead, his appeal is based on personal experience. Just as Paul was once a religious addict who came to discover true freedom in Christ, he now wants the Galatians to experience the same thing. Paul became like them—free from the law—and so they too should embrace this great freedom and let go of their unhealthy dependence on religion.

Years before, Jesus himself had shown us how humans are intended to live. He became like one of us in order to demonstrate that human beings are not victims of circumstance. On the contrary, we are victors because of the gift of God's salvation, and therefore we no longer need to live under the repressive rule of the law.

Paul also brings up something even more personal. He wrote,

---

1. Richard M. Sherman and Robert B. Sherman, *Mary Poppins: Vocal Selections from Walt Disney's* Mary Poppins, *Words and Music* (n.p.: Walt Disney Productions, 1984).

> You did not mistreat me when I first preached to you. Surely you remember that I was sick when I first brought you the good news. But even though my condition tempted you to reject me, you did not despise me or turn me away. No, you took me in and cared for me as though I were an angel from God or even Christ himself. (Gal 4:12–14)

From reading the New Testament, we can surmise that Paul was a man with many afflictions. Some afflictions were the result of persecution, but others seemed to be medical in nature. In this letter, he vulnerably discusses a particular sickness that he simply calls a "condition." The precise condition is not defined, and this ambiguity has caused many to speculate on what it might have been. The theories range from health issues (such as eye disease, malaria, epilepsy, and migraines) to depression or even mental anguish. We really can't know for sure. However, many agree that this condition is likely the thorn in the flesh that Paul mentions in another of his letters. Writing to the church in Corinth, he said,

> So to keep me from becoming proud, I was given a thorn in my flesh, a messenger from Satan to torment me and keep me from becoming proud. Three different times I begged the Lord to take it away. Each time he said, "My grace is all you need. My power is best in weakness." So now I am glad to boast about my weaknesses, so that the power of Christ can work through me. (2 Cor 12:7–9)

Whatever this condition was, it was enough for Paul to despise it. Yet through the grace of God, Paul embraced the Lord's ability to help him thrive in spite of it.

The ancients were much impressed by individuals who overcame personal infirmities to ultimately excel in areas of life that would otherwise seem improbable. Paul was one such person. Despite the thorn in his flesh, he was a tireless missionary, pastor, teacher, author, and world traveler.

These same ancients, however, were somewhat double-minded in that even though they admired such overcomers from a distance, they tended to shy away from people with medical conditions or abnormalities for fear that they might contract the same disease. But the Galatians were different. Even though Paul had a condition, they did not turn him away. Instead, they welcomed him with open arms and even went out of their way to take care of him. The care they gave was so gracious that they were said to treat Paul in much the same way they would have treated Christ himself.

In those days, messengers were given the same treatment that their sender would otherwise be given. That Paul was received well by the Galatians showed that they were completely open to Christ and the gospel message. Because of this, we can begin to understand why Paul was puzzled by the current behavior of the Galatians. The same people who heard and received the gospel were now reverting to their old ways, as if to reject the very gospel they once embraced. And not only were they back to where they had started, they had also apparently lost the joy that accompanied the blessing of redemption. This prompted Paul to write, "Where is that joyful and grateful spirit you felt then? I am sure you would have taken out your own eyes and given them to me if it had been possible" (Gal 4:15).

People who are addicted to religion are seldom joyful. They trudge through the motions of their religiosity with grim faces, often accompanied by murmuring or even desperate announcements of their piety. They are deeply religious but miserable, and rightly so. How can you expect people caught in a prison of faulty spirituality to be happy about anything? The Galatians were robbed of joy and it was evident in their behavior. They ceased to have the deep sense of gratitude that they once had when they first accepted the Gospel message. But in their backslidden state, they could not be thankful for anything because they were too busy working hard to make themselves pious.

I was once a religious addict surrounded by religious addicts. I went through the motions of going to church, observing the sacraments, upholding the Ten Commandments, and giving alms to the poor. Yet my life was void of joy. The word Paul used for "joy" literally means "blessedness." It's no wonder then that I had no joy. True spiritual blessedness does not come by working for one's own salvation. It comes by receiving God's free gift of eternal life by faith.

Interestingly, Paul noted how the Galatians used to live in such blessedness that they were even willing to take out their eyes in order to give them to him. This statement could substantiate the theory that Paul's "condition" was some kind of eye disease or defect. This reading, however, is in no way conclusive since the phrase "taken out your own eyes" could also be translated figuratively. The point being that they were so grateful to be blessed that they were willing to do anything to bless others. That is certainly good evidence of genuine spiritual growth and transformation.

But now, Paul was being treated like an antagonist. He asked the Galatians, "Have I now become your enemy because I am telling you the truth?"

(Gal 4:16). One of the favorite tools of a false teacher is flattery. Instead of telling us the truth, he or she will tell us what we want to hear. Naturally, we gravitate toward people who say such things. However, beware of the golden tongue. Many of history's greatest tragedies stemmed from the eloquence of madmen. Needless to say, the results have often been deadly. In his letter to Timothy, Paul warned, "For a time is coming when people will no longer listen to sound and wholesome teaching. They will follow their own desires and will look for teachers who will tell them whatever their itching ears want to hear. They will reject the truth and chase after myths" (2 Tim 4:3–4).

Paul, on the other hand, was not interested in competing in a popularity contest. He was not interested in being liked as much as he was intent on telling the truth. The truth, as we know, can hurt. And when people are immature, they resent being exposed to painful realities. Truth-tellers, therefore, always run the risk of being hated. But we must hate falsehood more, because the consequences of living in deceit are deadly. Because the Galatians lacked spiritual maturity, they turned against Paul because he painfully exposed the ugliness of their religious addiction.

Many years ago, I pointed out a weakness in the life of a friend. I tried to do it as lovingly as possible, but he still took offense. In fact, he was so upset with me that he refused to speak to me for quite a while. But in time, he realized that my motives were pure and that I only did what I did because I genuinely cared for him. Thankfully, our friendship is now restored, and he even expressed gratitude that I cared enough to tell him the truth.

Do not be afraid to be truthful. And be sure to speak truth in love. You may not always be appreciated at first, but in due time, the people we seek to help will hopefully mature and realize we were only looking out for their best interest. I know Paul certainly felt that way.

The Warning Against Enablers

Although individuals need to take responsibility for their addictive behavior, we know they cannot feed their addictions unless they are aided by enablers. For instance, there was a case in the Midwest where a man with an eating addiction ballooned to over eight hundred pounds. At his size, he was rendered immobile and was literally bedridden—yet he kept gaining weight. How so? Simple. His wife kept feeding him unhealthy meals in ridiculously large portions! She was his enabler.

The Galatians had their enablers too. Paul reminded them, "Those false teachers are so eager to win your favor, but their intentions are not good. They are trying to shut you off from me so that you will pay attention to them" (Gal 4:17). The Judaizers in Galatia were feeding the people a poor diet of lies and deceit. Because they were spiritually immature, the Galatians were gobbling it all up.

The Galatians were attracted to the false teachers because they appeared to be on their side. As Paul said, the wolves were eager to win the favor of these poor sheep. Eagerness, or zeal, can be a good quality. However, before we reward a person's eagerness, we must first understand what he or she is zealous about. In the case of the Judaizers, their zeal was misdirected because their motives and their teachings were not genuine.

I imagine that many, if not most, religious people are sincerely eager in their beliefs. As a result, we are often tolerant of other people's views because we figure that as long as they are sincere, they should be left alone. And while I truly appreciate the concept of tolerance, there is a point at which it can actually be a cop-out. Take the case of parents who are opposed to having their infants vaccinated. Although they may be sincere in their intent to protect their children, they are, in fact, leaving their children vulnerable to potentially life-threatening diseases. Sincerity and eagerness may be good qualities, but they do not guarantee the veracity of an act's merit. The act itself must be grounded in truth.

The Judaizers, however, were not only falsely eager, their very motives were also tainted. Their goal in teaching a deadly form of spirituality was based on the desire to alienate the Galatians from the Apostle Paul. The false teachers were flatterers, while Paul was a truth-teller. Flatterers are only after their own personal gain, while truth-tellers look out for the good of the people they love.

One way to distinguish between flatterers and truth-tellers is the demonstration of consistency. It's been said that if a man decides to be a liar, he had better have a good memory. The good thing about being truthful is that you don't have to remember what you said. Paul affirmed this principle when he wrote, "If someone is eager to do good things for you, that's all right; but let them do it all the time, not just when I'm with you" (Gal 4:18).

Some time ago, an investigative reporter ran a series of stories about people involved in deviant sexual behavior. His series was an incredible success. A few years later, however, the reporter himself was caught on video in a compromising situation with a woman who was not his wife! His hypocrisy got in the way of an otherwise compelling investigation series. It's not that the issue he covered in the news was unimportant but that his behavior was inconsistent with his message, which caused him to lose credibility in the eyes of the public.

If you are hooked on religion at the expense of righteousness, you need to identify the people who are enabling you to feed your addiction. Is your priest or pastor preaching the truth, or are they selling you a bunch of lies? Are your elders and deacons truly caring for the people, or are they using the church for financial gain? Are your gatherings marked by spiritual worship and genuine fellowship, or are they flimsy excuses for social snobbery and juicy gossip? Is your church a liberated community of people made righteous by Christ or is it a collection of incarcerated souls imprisoned by the chains of dead religiosity? While you are responsible for your religious addiction, understand that you also may be getting help from all the wrong people.

Enablers are hypocrites. They often claim to be concerned about people caught in addiction, but they do nothing to help the addict overcome their struggles. Even worse, enablers exhibit a degree of codependency when they go out of their way to help addicts (in the wrong way) in hopes that they will continue to be needed. In effect, enablers can become addicted to their own need to feel useful. Addiction is indeed a vicious cycle that quickly spirals out of control. The only hope is to seek the help of the Almighty God.

The Appeal for Personal Responsibility

Paul was no stranger to religious addiction, for he himself was once caught in this venomous lifestyle. His religious credentials were impeccable. Consider the résumé he submitted to the Philippian believers:

> I was circumcised when I was eight days old. I am a pure-blooded citizen of Israel and a member of the tribe of Benjamin—a real Hebrew if there ever was one! I was a member of the Pharisees, who demand the strictest obedience to the Jewish law. I was so zealous that I harshly persecuted the church. And as for righteousness, I obeyed the law without fault. (Phil 3:5–6)

I doubt that many of us could contend with these superb qualifications. Yet when Paul was faced with the truth of the gospel, he willingly rid himself of all these credentials for the sake of Christ. Paul lost his religion, as he confessed: "I once thought these things were valuable, but now I consider them worthless because of what Christ has done" (Phil 3:7). It's no wonder Paul was so adamant about helping the Galatians with their addiction. He personally understood the joy that came with the abandonment of false beliefs in exchange for the glorious blessing of salvation by grace through faith. It broke his heart to see the Galatians voluntarily returning to a life of religious imprisonment after they had already heard the truth.

Paul also knew there was only so much he could do. He could try to persuade the Galatians, but in the end, they would have to make the choice themselves. The fact that Paul was far away from Galatia made it even more difficult for him, as he wrote,

> Oh, my dear children! I feel as if I'm going through labor pains for you again, and they will continue until Christ is fully developed in your lives. I wish I were with you right now so I could change my tone. But at this distance I don't know how else to help you. (Gal 4:19–20)

Reverting back to a parental stance, Paul is making another strong appeal for the Galatians to come back to the truth. The imagery of childbirth is an especially powerful one. If you have ever seen a woman give birth, you will marvel at the amount of energy expended—through painful labor—to bring a child out into the world. Paul's wish for the Galatians is that they would not only come to life, but that they would also continue to grow and develop in their relationship with Jesus Christ. To say *no* to religious narcotics requires that you say *yes* to Christ. And that is a decision each person must make for him or herself. Paul wished he could do more, but considering how distant he was from the Galatians, writing them a forceful letter was the best he could do. Where the Galatians would go from there was completely up to them.

When I was doing ministry in the Philippines, our church began a ministry to help people recover from drug addiction. A few years after this ministry was launched, it became apparent that the recovery rate of those who entered the program was remarkably high. After a period of assessing outcomes, it was suggested a major factor in the program's success was the subjects' personal resolve to change. Unlike other programs where people forcibly turned in their sons and daughters for rehabilitation, our program only took in people who turned themselves in. Unless the addicted individual was willing to take personal responsibility for his or her addiction, there was no sense in trying to help them overcome their weakness.

Fooling Ourselves with Fig Leaves

If today you find yourself hopelessly addicted to religion, learn the lesson that the Galatians had to painfully learn for themselves. Religion does not set you free; rather, it imprisons you. You need to seek real change, because otherwise your addiction will get the best of you. Enablers are not your friends; they are part of the problem. Ultimately, you cannot blame anyone but yourself, for you have to be personally responsible for the life you chose to live. Are you willing to lose your religion in order to gain the blessing of righteousness through God's amazing grace? That's a question only you can answer.

9

Two Is a Crowd

Galatians 4:21–5:1

Some days, life resembles a sitcom, while other days it feels more like a soap opera. I grew up with two brothers and, for the most part, we usually got along. One of the things we love to do together is laugh—and if you added my dad to the mix, there was sure to be a riot! Once in a while, however, we would get on each other's nerves. When we don't get along with our siblings, we often feel that Mom and Dad had one too many children. I imagine the same would be true in any household, even in the ancient world. This was certainly the case with the family of Abraham.

Abraham is one of the most beloved figures in the Bible. His is a story of faith of the highest order. But it was also a life of struggle, tension, testing, and yes, family discord. We could label his story, which is recorded in the book of Genesis, as an ancient soap opera. In his attempt to expose the false teachings that had plagued the church in Galatia, the Apostle Paul uses the story of Abraham to drive home an important point. It is important, therefore, to be familiar with the story before we try to understand Paul's point.

Without getting into too much detail, let's examine the part of Abraham's life that has to do with God's promise to make him the father of a great nation. Roughly two thousand years before the birth of Jesus, God commanded Abraham to leave his native country of Ur for a new land. In this promised land, God said, "I will make you into a great nation . . . I will bless you and make you famous, and you will be a blessing to others" (Gen 12:2). So Abraham obeyed God.

In order to appreciate the depth of Abraham's obedience, it helps to know that at the time he heard God's promise, he was already seventy-five years old. As if that were not enough, he and his wife, Sarah (who was old enough to start collecting social security), did not have any children. Indeed, Sarah was barren! So there you have it: an old and childless couple leaving the comforts of home in order to start a new life . . . and a new family.

Fast-forward a decade, and the couple remains childless. They were becoming impatient, so Sarah came up with a plan. There was a custom in those days by which a barren wife would offer her maidservant to her husband for the purpose of bearing a child. Perhaps Sarah figured that God promised to make Abraham a father but never specified that she would be the mother. So according to Gen 16, Sarah asked her husband to use her Egyptian servant, Hagar, as a surrogate mother—and Abraham agreed. In time, Hagar became with child.

Unfortunately, Sarah would come to regret this decision. Once Hagar was pregnant, she started to treat Sarah with scorn (Gen 16:4). With Abraham's consent, Sarah began mistreating Hagar, causing the pregnant servant to run away. The Lord, however, convinced Hagar to return with a submissive attitude. He even promised to bless Hagar with many descendants (Gen 16:10). So she returned, and when the time came, she gave birth to Abraham's son. He was named Ishmael, meaning "God hears," because God heard Hagar's cry of distress.

There you have it. Abraham now had a son! But remember, this is a soap opera, so to end now would make it too easy. As it turned out, God had in fact intended for Sarah, not Hagar, to be the mother of Abraham's promised child. When Abraham was ninety years old, God reiterated his promise to make Abraham the father of a great nation. And as a sign of this covenant, the Lord commanded that every male in this new nation should be circumcised. With this, God said, "Your bodies will bear the mark of my everlasting covenant . . . Any male who fails to be circumcised will be cut off from the covenant family for breaking the covenant" (Gen 17:13-14).

Several years would pass before the promise would come to fruition. But this time, Abraham and Sarah chose to be patient. In Gen 18, we are told that God's messengers visited the aging couple. One of them said, "I will return to you about this time next year, and your wife, Sarah, will have a son" (Gen 18:10). Sarah laughed in seeming disbelief. But sure enough, even though she was well past childbearing age, Sarah miraculously gave birth to a son a year later. They named the boy Isaac, meaning "he laughs," for he brought joy and laughter to Abraham's household.

The drama, however, was not over. When Isaac and Ishmael were a little older, Sarah witnessed Ishmael bullying his younger half-brother, Isaac. She demanded that Hagar and Ishmael be sent away. Furthermore, she said, "He [Ishmael] is not going to share the inheritance with my son, Isaac" (Gen 21:10). And so Hagar and Ishmael were sent away. But God did not forget them. Although it was through Isaac that God was to create a promised nation, Ishmael would himself be the father of a great nation (Gen 21:18). That is why to this very day Jewish people and Arabic people point to a common ancestry in Abraham—the Jews through Isaac and the Arabs through Ishmael. Ironically, the sibling rivalry remains alive and strong.

Let's return to Paul's letter to the Galatians. The apostle uses this portion of Abraham's story to illustrate his point regarding the law and the promise. The illustration is effective because the Judaizers in Galatia would have been thoroughly familiar with Abraham's story. In fact, they had misused this illustration to show why the circumcised descendants of Abraham were spiritually superior to those who were not marked accordingly. Paul, on the other hand, offers a very different perspective.

The remainder of Gal 4 marks the end of Paul's diatribe. This time, Paul employs an illustration based on contrasts. In this case, a contrast between the two sons, the two mothers, the two spiritual identities, and the two destinies that face all of humanity.

Two Sons

In ancient diatribes, it was common to set up an imaginary opponent with whom to carry on an argument. Paul does this when he begins this part of the argument by saying, "Tell me, you who want to live under the law, do you know what the law actually says?" (Gal 4:21). With these words, Paul was forcing his opponents to think about whether or not they really understood the core of their assertion. This is an important point, because if we do not deal with the central issue, we end up ranting about peripheral matters that distract us from what is important. For instance, I often hear people asking God for more patience. But do you really know what you are asking for when you utter such a prayer? The only way God can give you patience is by putting you in a situation where your patience will be tested and, hopefully, proven. So in essence, when you say, "God, give me patience," you are actually saying, "God, put me in a situation that will cause my patience to emerge." But we often don't realize this. In fact, we complain when life gets tough without understanding that this may very well have been the answer to our prayer.

Perhaps the Galatians had not fully grasped the implications of living under the law. When Paul asked them, "Do you know what the law actually says?" he was really asking if they knew what it meant. I am certain the Judaizers could have recited the Ten Commandments, as well as other stipulations, word for word. But knowing a commandment and understanding it are two different things. As my friend would often say, "I not only know all the Ten Commandments, I've broken every one of them!"

By asking the Galatians about the law, Paul was not limiting his discussion to the Decalogue. Rather, he seemed to be referring to the larger body of Scripture known as the Law (Torah). We know this because he is about to refer to the Abraham story, which predates the giving of the Ten Commandments and yet falls well within the parameters of the Torah.

Referring to the Genesis narrative, Paul wrote, "The Scriptures say that Abraham had two sons, one from his slave wife and one from his freeborn wife" (Gal 4:22). The fact is, Abraham had more than two sons. Sometime after the death of his first wife, Sarah, "Abraham married another wife, whose name was Keturah . . . She gave birth to Zimran, Jokshan, Medan, Midian, Ishbak, and Shuah" (Gen 25:1-2). Why, then, does Paul say that Abraham had two sons? The key is to notice what Paul did not say. Paul does not say Abraham had *only* two sons. Clearly, he had more. But for the purpose of Paul's argument, only Isaac and Ishmael were significant enough to make his point; therefore, he focuses only on them.

Interestingly, Paul does not mention Abraham's sons by name; rather, he identifies them using their maternal parentage. The son we know as Ishmael is described as the "one from his slave wife," while the son we know as Isaac is described as the "one from his freeborn wife." There was no doubt that both were fully Abraham's sons, but the rank of each son was determined by his mother's status. Identity is a funny thing, isn't it? We tend to describe ourselves based on who we are in relation to others. For instance, the only reason I can call myself a father is because I have children. I am only a husband because I have a spouse. I couldn't possibly be a teacher unless I had students (otherwise I would only be a talkative fool). In the same way, Abraham's two sons each carried a unique identity because of who their mothers were. Hagar was a slave; therefore, Ishmael was a child of slavery. Sarah was a freewoman; therefore, Isaac was a child of freedom. And because each had a different status, each son also had a different inheritance.

Ironically, although the Judaizers in Galatia would have identified with Isaac, Paul argues that they were actually following the path of Ishmael. As he explains, "The son of the slave wife was born in a human attempt to bring about the fulfillment of God's promise . . . But the son of the freeborn was born as God's own fulfillment of his promise" (Gal 4:23). When Sarah and Abraham were getting impatient with the promise of God, they decided to speed things up by using Hagar as a surrogate mother. The problem was, surrogate motherhood was not part of God's plan. What Abraham and Sarah did was fundamentally the same as Adam and Eve covering themselves with fig leaves. Both the leaves and the surrogate were human attempts to do what only God can do. They are powerful forms of vain religiosity. Religion, in the worst sense of the word, is an exercise in futility because no righteousness is gained as a result of it. God rejected the use of the fig leaves, he rejected the use of a surrogate mother, and he continues to reject our vain religions.

The promise of God is born out of the will and the ways of God. What made Isaac unique was that his birth was a result of God's own fulfillment of his promise. Even as he rejected Adam and Eve's fig leaves, the Lord provided animal skin to cover their nakedness. He rejected the plan of surrogate motherhood, and in its place miraculously gave Abraham and Sarah a son of their own. In the same way, God rejects our futile religions and instead provides us with his one and only Son, Jesus, who died for our sins and blesses us with the gifts of righteousness and eternal life.

Although the Judaizers were physically of the line of Isaac, they were spiritually of the line of Ishmael. As such, their religious adherence to the law could never help them attain the righteousness of God. It was important for Paul to help the foolish Galatian believers realize this ironic folly.

Two Women

This time, Paul shifts his focus to the mothers of Abraham's two sons. By contrasting Sarah and Hagar, Paul continues to expose the difference between living by the law and living by grace. He writes, "These two women serve as an illustration of God's two covenants. The first woman, Hagar, represents Mount Sinai, where people received the law that enslaved them" (Gal 4:24).

This short passage is filled with several important symbols found in the Old Testament. Paul uses the story of Sarah and Hagar to illustrate the two agreements made by God. Hagar, the enslaved woman, represents the covenant of the law. The giving of the law on Mount Sinai serves as the covenantal foundation for Judaism, while the death of Jesus on the cross is the covenantal foundation for Christianity. Although the giving of the law was a monumental event in the history of God's people, the law itself does not accomplish what some think it does. Specifically, the Judaizers taught that obedience to the law was a means by which we gain the favor of God. Although Paul already made this point earlier in his letter, clearly he felt this was such a crucial flaw in the Galatian heresy that it warranted another mention. Not only does the law show us that we are sinners, it also enslaves us to its unattainable demands for perfect holiness. Since no one can make him or herself holy, no one can break free from the sentence imposed by the words of the law.

I am reminded of a driver I know in the Philippines who wrecked his delivery truck due to sheer carelessness. The truck was beyond repair, so the company had to buy a new one. As part of the driver's reprimand, his boss said, "We will deduct money out of your monthly paycheck until this new truck is fully paid off." Realizing that it would probably take his entire lifetime to pay off the truck, the driver knew he would be enslaved as an employee of that company forever. So to the boss' surprise, he responded, "Oh boy! Job security!" Unfortunately, unlike this driver's situation, enslavement to the law is no laughing matter.

Paul goes on to say, "And now Jerusalem is just like Mount Sinai in Arabia, because she and her children live in slavery to the law" (Gal 4:25). The Galatian readers would have been familiar with this geographic reference. The region known as Arabia included the famous Mount Sinai, the site where the law was given to Moses. In the first century, the inhabitants of Arabia were the Nabataean Arabs. It so happens that these people traced their ancestry all the way back to Ishmael. Although the Judaizers would have associated Mount Sinai with the Mosaic covenant, Paul asserts that in its present situation, it is more closely associated with the lineage of Ishmael and, consequently, his mother Hagar.

In contrast to Hagar is Isaac's mother, Sarah. Paul said, "But the other woman, Sarah, represents the heavenly Jerusalem. She is the free woman, and she is our mother" (Gal 4:26). In the Bible, the word "Jerusalem" is a multi-faceted term that can symbolize many things. Literally, it is the most important city in Jewish culture. Allegorically, it can refer to the church. Prophetically, it is used as a reference to the heavenly city that God will once again establish for his people. John the Beloved caught a glimpse of this and recorded it in the last book of the Bible. He wrote,

> Then I saw a new heaven and a new earth, for the old heaven and the old earth had disappeared. And the sea was also gone. And I saw the holy city, the new Jerusalem, coming down from God out of heaven like a bride beautifully dressed for her husband. (Rev 21:1–2)

Although their vision of the future may not have been as vivid as John's, many first-century Jews were, in fact, looking forward to the hope offered by the coming of this new Jerusalem. While Paul would agree that the new Jerusalem was yet to come, he seems to assert that in a spiritual sense, the blessing of Jerusalem is already realized in the person of Jesus Christ. Furthermore, Sarah and Jerusalem share a common symbolism in that both are viewed as mothers. Sarah is the mother of the faithful, while Jerusalem is the mother of the people of God. Just as Sarah was born free, those who believe in the Lord Jesus Christ are born again as freed people.

Paul concludes this part of the illustration by quoting a passage from the book of Isaiah:

> As Isaiah said,
>
> "Rejoice, O childless woman,
>   you who have never given birth!
> Break into a joyful shout,
>   you who have never been in labor!
> For the desolate woman now has more children
>   than the woman who lives with her husband!"

This passage, taken from Isa 54:1, was originally a prophecy that referred to the restoration of Jerusalem after a time of exile. According to Isaiah, the people of Jerusalem would experience more prosperity after the city was restored compared to before to the exile. Paul's reference to this prophecy is appropriate in that the blessing of salvation (based on promise) that follows the death of Christ is far greater than any other blessing (based on law) received before Jesus died.

Coincidentally, the Jewish people often associated Isaiah's prophecy with the pregnancy of Sarah. Just as God restored Sarah's barren womb with the gift of a child, they believed God would also restore Israel after a time of great suffering and distress. The Judaizers, however, did not take the symbolism far enough. They failed to push the analogy further by omitting the fact that the full restoration of the human soul comes through the suffering and death of Jesus Christ. Void of this realization, the Judaizers instead continued to enslave the people by teaching them to remain subject to the law.

Two Identities

Paul accused the Judaizers of being spiritual Ishmaelites, children of the slave woman and, consequently, people enslaved by the law. But what about the rest of the people in Galatia? Were they enslaved as well? Maybe not yet, but they were treading a dangerous path. Paul wanted the Galatians to grasp this and therefore writes, "And you, dear brothers and sisters, are children of the promise, just like Isaac" (Gal 4:28). There was no doubt in Paul's mind that the Galatians had genuinely received Christ in their hearts upon hearing the gospel the first time. That they were now exposed to false teachings did not automatically mean they had lost their initial blessing, only that they were in danger of living substandard spiritual lives if they continued following the Judaizers.

The false teachers had insisted that the continued practice of circumcision was necessary in order to reap the blessings of salvation. But Paul made it clear that salvation was not a result of a religious ritual. In his letter to the Romans, Paul wrote, "for not all who are born into the nation of Israel are truly members of God's people! Being descendants of Abraham doesn't make them truly Abraham's children" (Rom 9:6–7). Paul continued to refer to the Galatians as believers (brothers and sisters), recognizing their unity in the family of God. But by also calling them "children of the promise," Paul quickly reminded the Galatians that their status as God's children was based neither on their national identity nor on their obedience to the law but on the fulfilled promise of God.

As a young man, people told me that I was a Christian because I was baptized as an infant. Supposedly, this beautiful ritual was the reason I had become part of the Christian family. After some time and as a result of searching the Scriptures, I came to understand that although infant baptism indeed made me a member of a religious institution, it neither made me a child of God nor a follower of Jesus Christ. Ritual baptism and genuine conversion are two different, mutually exclusive experiences. To think otherwise would be to make the same mistake the Judaizers made. To be truly righteous, I had to lose my trust in myself and in an earthly institution to instead put my faith in the power, the grace, and the gift of God through

Jesus Christ. No institution or person, including myself, could ever make me righteous. Only Christ could do that.

It has been said that if you wish to avoid controversy, you should refrain from discussing politics and religion. We hold on dearly to our ideologies—so much so that when our beliefs are attacked, we take it personally. This was certainly true among the believers in Galatia. Paul said, "But you are now being persecuted by those who want you to keep the law, just as Ishmael, the child born by human effort, persecuted Isaac, the child born by the power of the Spirit" (Gal 4:29). As it turned out, the Judaizers were harassing the Galatian believers who upheld the doctrine of justification by faith alone. According to Paul, this was reminiscent of how Ishmael had harassed his younger half-brother Isaac. Based on the Genesis account, Sarah was dismayed when she saw Ishmael "making fun of her son, Isaac" (Gen 21:9).

Persecution is a type of bullying. It can come in the form of teasing, which may often seem harmless but can cause a tremendous amount of pain, inconvenience, and in some cases even death. Interestingly, the persecution in Galatia was perpetrated by those who were devoutly religious. Let's not forget that even Jesus was harassed by religious people. I find it ironic that the most religious among us can also be the most miserable and the most hostile—a living paradox if there ever was one.

In my work as a pastor, I continue to be amused by how some of the most challenging people are not those outside of the church but those within it. Often, people come to church with their own agendas or their own view of what constitutes true spirituality. The activists among them can be a burden to those who don't see things their way. Needless to say, modern Judaizers are alive and well even in twenty-first-century churches.

It was important for Paul to call out the Judaizers because there was a danger that even the faithful in Galatia might eventually become sympathetic to the wrong cause. In psychology, we refer to this phenomenon as Stockholm Syndrome. The term was coined by a criminologist named Nils Bejerot and is based on a bank robbery that took place in Stockholm, Sweden. The hostages in the bank were held for six days. During this time, many of the hostages became emotionally attached to the bank robbers and even defended them after the ordeal was over. Although Paul was obviously not familiar with this modern term, he was clearly aware of the phenomenon. The longer the Galatians were exposed to false teachers, the greater the possibility that they would become sympathetic to the Judaizers and therefore apathetic to Paul's gospel message. This is also why people who are trapped in ungodly cults can be difficult to rescue. They have been brainwashed into believing so many lies that the truth is no longer recognizable to them. Paul had to grip the hearts of the Galatians before it was too late.

What, then, does Paul recommend the Galatians do? He instructs them by saying, "But what do the Scriptures say about that? 'Get rid of the slave and her son, for the son of the slave woman will not share the inheritance with the free woman's son'" (Gal 4:30). Those words first came out of the mouth of Sarah (Gen 21:10), who told Abraham to get rid of Hagar and her son after discovering Ishmael was bullying Isaac. Paul was telling the Galatian believers to reject the Judaizers and their false teachings by getting rid of them. They were a poison to the church that had to be removed. The harshness of Paul's command was a commentary on how seriously dangerous these false teachers were. This was not a time to play nice, for the venom had to be removed immediately.

If by "religion" we mean the act of loving God and caring for others, then there is certainly nothing wrong with that. But remember that Paul is speaking of religiosity in terms of the vain human attempt to seek righteousness apart from the grace of God. In this case, religiosity and righteousness are incompatible. The law of physics that says no two objects can occupy the exact same space at the exact same time has a spiritual counterpart. The human heart only has room for either religion or righteousness; the two cannot coexist in the same space. And if you choose God's righteousness through faith, then you must necessarily rid yourself of the other.

Two Paths

Paul ends his diatribe by making two conclusions, both marked by the word "so." He writes, "So, dear brothers and sisters, we are not children of the slave woman; we are children of the free woman. So Christ has truly set us free. Now make sure that you stay free, and don't get tied up again in slavery to the law" (Gal 4:31–5:1). Once again, Paul addresses the believers as "brothers and sisters" in order to make it clear that they were not to be associated with the false teachers among them. Furthermore, he uses the term "we" instead of "you." That is, they were not on the side of the Judaizers. Instead, they were part of Paul. Unlike the Judaizers, who were children of Hagar, true believers are children of Sarah.

It is important to remind people who they are. Whenever we attend a social function, we give our three children the same speech before we get out of the car. Ana or I will say, "Kids, once we enter this home, we expect you to be at your best behavior. Do not do or say anything that will reflect poorly on who we are as a family. Remember, you are Micianos." Sometimes, our children would ask, "But how come the other kids don't need to behave like we do?" Our answer would be simple but to the point: "Those kids are not our concern because they are not our children." In time, all three of them got the point.

Caring for them as his own spiritual children, Paul admonished each Galatian believer to behave as one who is liberated by Christ. As an added reminder, he told them to not get trapped in a manner of thinking that once enslaved them. Once we get a taste of freedom, we are not to carelessly wander into situations where that precious gift might ever be compromised.

In the Midwest, there is a train station where two tracks run parallel to each other. They appear to be following the exact same path. But if you follow one track, you will end up in New York, and if you follow the other, you will end up in California. Interesting, isn't it? Two paths that look identical at first actually lead to very different destinations. Sometimes religiosity and righteousness can appear to run parallel. It doesn't seem to make any difference which path we take. But we soon learn that nothing could be farther from the truth. The path of religiosity leads to imprisonment, while the path of righteousness leads to freedom. It is therefore incumbent upon us to choose our path wisely.

In 2010, I chanced upon an interesting book entitled *The Other Wes Moore: One Name and Two Fates—A Story of Tragedy and Hope*. As the title suggests, it is a book about a man named Wes Moore. Wes had a rather rough start in life, but he eventually blossomed into a man of honor. He served as a paratrooper in the United States Army, was educated in Oxford as a Rhodes Scholar, and currently works as a finance analyst for Citigroup. While getting ready to study in Oxford, he discovered there was another man by the name of Wes Moore. Ironically, they both grew up in the same neighborhood. However, unlike him, the other Wes Moore was a criminal who was sentenced to prison for killing a police officer. Wes started to write to the other Wes, striking up an interesting correspondence that went on for some time. He wrote the book based on this interchange of letters with the other Wes.

It's remarkable how two men with the same exact name, despite growing up in the same neighborhood, could end up living such different lives. There are many people who label themselves "spiritual." But not all spirituality is the same. Although they can sometimes sound alike, look alike, and feel alike, a spirituality based on human religion results in spiritual incarceration, while a spirituality based on faith in Christ leads to righteousness, freedom, and eternal life. When it comes to deciding whether it is religion or righteousness that will saturate our hearts and minds, you will discover that two is definitely a crowd, for there is only room for one.

10

Take It or Leave It
Galatians 5:2–15

ADVICE IS ONLY AS good as the recipient's willingness to heed it. In the summer of 2011, the CEO of a video service company was having a casual conversation with a friend. He shared his plans to expand the business by splitting his current service into two separate departments, each with a different billing system. His friend advised him not to do it, but the CEO went ahead with his plan anyway. Within a few weeks, the company lost 800,000 customers who were dissatisfied with the decision. As it turned out, the friend's advice was sound, but it was still up to the CEO to take it or leave it.

In this portion of his letter to the Galatians, Paul is about to offer some advice. So far, he had been developing a theological foundation for asserting the doctrine of justification by faith. Now, Paul begins this new section by spelling out the practical implications of this doctrine. Paul will devote the rest of his letter to teaching righteous people how to behave righteously. He is mindful that it will still be up to the Galatians whether or not to heed his advice, but he will certainly do his best to make a compelling argument.

It is not unusual for Paul to divide his letters into two parts, with a doctrinal assertion followed by practical commitments. The order in which Paul presents these parts is no coincidence. Theology precedes ethics, not the other way around. Unfortunately, it doesn't always work that way in modern culture. In fact, in many cases, people get it wrong. People behave a certain way, then conclude that that is an acceptable way to live. The result of this kind of thinking is, unfortunately, often tragic. Take, for instance, a culture that tolerates lying. At some point, speaking deceitfully becomes commonplace as people come to assume that everyone does it. In time, lying becomes so fully integrated in such a society that people simply accept it as a fact of life—and some may even be proud of it!

Some might read the last two chapters of this epistle and say, "Nobody lives like this!" Perhaps. Paul, however, is not giving his advice based on what is but rather on what should be. He acknowledges that believers—including himself—struggle to live godly lives. But that struggle should not keep us from striving to live on a higher plane. Furthermore, we who believe are blessed with the gift of the Holy Spirit, who is in the business of transforming us into the likeness of Christ, so that by yielding to him, we continue to grow in God's righteousness with each passing day.

Paul begins this section on practical commitments with a series of brief but persuasive instructions.

Take All or Nothing

If I didn't believe in God, I would think Abraham lost his marbles. Think about it. If someone said to you, "God told me to remove your genital foreskin," would you let them do it? Yet that's exactly what happened, according to the book of Genesis. As a sign of his covenant with Abraham, the Lord said,

> Your responsibility is to obey the terms of the covenant. You and all your descendants have this continual responsibility. This is the covenant that you and your descendants must keep: Each male among you must be circumcised. You must cut off the flesh of your foreskin as a sign of the covenant between me and you. From generation to generation, every male child must be circumcised on the eighth day after his birth. This applies not only to members of your family, but also to the servants born in your household and the foreign-born servants whom you have purchased. All must be circumcised. Your bodies will bear the mark of my everlasting covenant. Any male who fails to be circumcised will be cut off from the covenant family for breaking the covenant. (Gen 17:9–14)

Since that time, Jews have continued the practice of circumcision. By the time Paul was writing to the Galatians, the Judaizers not only viewed circumcision as a sign of the covenant, they also insisted it was a requirement for righteousness. Obviously, Paul disagreed. He told the Galatians, "Listen! I Paul tell you this: If you are counting on circumcision to make you right with God, then Christ will be of no benefit to you" (Gal 5:2). After opening with the emphatic "Listen!" Paul insists that the way of the law and the way of Christ are diametrically opposed to each other and that only one of them leads to true righteousness.

First of all, let's be clear on what Paul is not saying. He is not asserting that circumcision is a bad thing or even that it was ever a bad idea. He himself was circumcised as an infant. And before launching on his second missionary journey, he had his apprentice, Timothy, circumcised (Acts 16:3). As a conscientious Jew, Paul understood the historical significance of the practice of circumcision.

Paul's understanding of circumcision was totally unlike the way others viewed it. For instance, according to the *Historia Augusta* (a collection of biographies on the lives of Roman emperors), the emperor Hadrian issued a decree banning the practice of circumcision. Some even believe this decree played a role in the Bar Kokhba revolt of AD 132. Even in modern history, the medical practice of circumcision continues to be debated. Not long ago, arguing that circumcision is tantamount to child mutilation, residents of San Francisco proposed a citywide ban on the practice. Although the measure did not make it to the ballot, the debate continues.

Paul did not have a problem with circumcision as a sign of the Abrahamic covenant. After all, this was a biblical and historical fact. What was problematic was the insistence that circumcision was a prerequisite for righteousness, even for Gentiles (for whom the practice was culturally and historically irrelevant). In the first century, there were some Jews who believed that Gentiles could be saved by simply observing the seven laws given to Noah after the flood (Gen 9). Others, however, insisted on fully observing all the laws found in the Old Testament, specifically, the Mitzvot (a collection of 613 commandments found throughout the Torah, the writings of Moses). Religious symbols are not necessarily wrong, as long as we acknowledge the limitations of what they represent. Circumcision was a God-ordained symbol of his covenant, but it was never a means of attaining righteousness. Anyone who thought otherwise missed the point and, consequently, failed to reap the benefits of Christ's sacrifice on the cross.

Making his point even more emphatically, Paul wrote,

> I'll say it again. If you are trying to find favor with God by being circumcised, you must obey every regulation in the whole law of Moses. For if you are trying to make yourselves right with God by keeping the law, you have been cut off from Christ! You have fallen away from God's grace. (Gal 5:3–4)

Seeking salvation through circumcision was indicative of a type of legalism, and legalism is a horribly harsh taskmaster. Void of any notion of grace, legalism operated on an all-or-nothing proposition. Either you obey all of the law or you obey nothing at all. To obey most of the law while faltering in even one respect is to nullify all your attempts at becoming righteous.

That is why Paul said, "If you are trying to find favor with God by being circumcised, you must obey every regulation of the whole law of Moses." This all-or-nothing mentality is actually considered a psychological disorder. Specifically, it is a cognitive distortion because it is based on exaggeration and irrational thinking. Take the case of a straight-A student who gets back her project report only to find it marked with a grade of B. It is not unusual for such a person to fall into a state of self-deprecation and say, "I am such an idiot; I can't believe I could be so stupid!" Frankly, I would have been ecstatic to get a B anytime, but Ms. Straight-A over here is of a different sort (I'm sure you've all met her before). She has fooled herself into believing she should either get a perfect grade or no grade at all. The absence of any middle ground totally distorts her sense of value as a student and as a person.

That's the problem with legalism: you must perfectly obey all the law because nothing else is acceptable. The problem is that nobody, not even your sweet grandmother, is capable of perfectly obeying *every* law in the Bible. So what is the alternative? Paul said that by following the path of legalism, you cut yourself off from Christ. Conversely, the path of grace is forgiving. It acknowledges that no individual can perfectly follow the requirements of God. But we need not worry, because even our shortcomings do not undo the work of the cross. Salvation is based solely on the merits of Christ's redemptive work, not on our attempt or ability to fulfill the requirements of the law.

Paul has an amusing knack for wordplay. He said that those who try to attain righteousness through legalism are "cut off from Christ." The term "cut off" is drawn from the imagery of circumcision. In this case, the removal of the foreskin is a graphic euphemism for separation from Christ. As a result, the legalist has "fallen away from God's grace." I don't think Paul was teaching the Galatians that believers can lose their salvation. Rather, he was letting them know that if they decided to align themselves along the path of legalism, they would be stepping outside the realm of God's grace—much like a train that jumps off the track and veers away from the path graciously engineered to lead it safely toward a particular destination. It would be utterly wasteful to have had received the gift of salvation by grace through faith only to go on living according to the old ways of religiosity and legalism. Why continue to pay for something that is already freely given to you?

The failure to appreciate gifts is a great tragedy indeed. Earlier this year, our church participated in a festival hosted by our city. We set up a booth where our volunteers handed out all kinds of free stuff to everyone who wanted them—things like balloons, candy, and bottled water. During my shift, a man walked up to our booth and asked how much a bottle of water was. "It's free," I said. Yet he pulled out a dollar, insisting that he pay for it. "You don't have to pay me," I responded. "Just take it." The guy wouldn't budge. He grabbed a bottle of water, shoved the dollar in my hand, then walked away. I felt like such an awful communicator. I mean, what part of "free" did he not understand? He unnecessarily paid for something he could have enjoyed at no cost. As far as I was concerned, a simple "thank you" would have been enough.

I, on the other hand, like free stuff (don't judge me; I have Filipino blood). Birthdays are especially exciting. Whenever I invite people to my birthday party, I tell them to just walk up to our front door and ring the doorbell with their elbows. If they ask why, I jokingly say, "You don't plan to come empty-handed, do you?" Let's face it: gifts are awesome! All that great stuff that you only dream of—and it's all free! Well, free to you, that is. But don't misinterpret "free" for "cheap." Unlike that cheap toy that comes with a Happy Meal, the gift of eternal life is far from worthless. In fact, it came at the price of Jesus' very own life. The gift is not cheap, but it is paid for. All we have to do is accept it with gratitude. Any attempt to pay for it would be a horrible insult to the Giver.

Live by the Spirit

Paul now presents a striking contrast between those who take the way of the law versus those who go by the way of faith. He writes, "But we who live by the Spirit eagerly wait to receive by faith the righteousness God has promised to us" (Gal 5:5). When he says, "but we," Paul includes himself among those who reject legalism and embrace faith. What is interesting is the way he now describes the believer. He uses four descriptive terms to point out the differences between the legalist and the righteous.

First, he says that righteous people "live by the Spirit." Unlike legalists, who are prisoners to living by the law, the Christian has such a personal relationship with God that the Spirit is able to lead him or her in a way of life that glorifies the Savior. Rather than living like a train bound by a pre-constructed track, the believer lives in total freedom. Freedom, however, does not mean we are liberated to do as we wish; rather, it means we are empowered to do as we ought. We could not do that under the law because, as the law revealed, we were bound by our sinful nature, and as a result, we could not help but do only what that nature desired. When we are addicted to our sinful way of life, it might seem like we are rebelling against God by our own free will, but in reality we are only doing what our fallen nature is forcing us to do. When we live by the Spirit, we are transformed into beings capable of doing the very things we were originally created to do. In this sense, we are truly free.

Second, we are people who "eagerly await." Legalists are impatient people. They want instant gratification for every sacrificial act. Unable to wait for God to fulfill his promise, they manipulate events to realize their hopes, even if it means doing so outside the realm of God's will. But righteous people live by the Spirit, and one of the fruits of the Spirit is patience. Anything worth having is worth waiting for. We can certainly wait eagerly for God's promises, but we must wait nonetheless. If we let our eagerness get in the way of patience, things go wrong. Imagine a person who can't wait for a cake to bake. He or she might be tempted to take the cake out of the oven prematurely only to find that it cannot be enjoyed properly half-baked. Sometimes, or perhaps many times, it just makes more sense to wait.

Third, we wait "by faith." Legalists cannot wait, and therefore they tend to do things on their own rather than trust in the Lord. Faith, on the other hand, involves learning to trust in God even in the absence of any immediate, tangible evidence. The author of Hebrews put it this way: "Faith is the confidence that what we hope for will actually happen; it gives us assurance about things we cannot see" (Gal 11:1). Before you argue that this is difficult to put into practice, may I suggest that you actually do this all the time? Take your job, for instance. You go to work day after day, yet at the end of each day, you don't get paid. That doesn't stop you from going back to work the next day. Why? Because you have faith that every fifteen days, you will get the paycheck your employer promised you. He doesn't dangle the check in front of you as you work; he simply gives you his word. In effect, you have believed in something you cannot see. Your employer's words, whether given verbally or in a written contract, are sufficient for you to do your job without worrying about where your pay will come from. Likewise, God's Word is yes and amen. If God makes a promise, we believe it will be fulfilled at the right time. Meanwhile, we simply eagerly wait for it to come.

Fourth, we wait for the "righteousness that God has promised." Legalists do not seek the righteousness of God as much as they seek their own self-created piety. Much like the Pharisees who flaunt their spirituality—publicly giving alms to the poor and praying aloud so that everyone hears them—the legalist is more interested in the attention of others rather than the approval of God. Jesus warned us against such a vile way of thinking. He said,

> When you pray, don't babble on and on as people of other religions do. They think their prayers are answered merely by repeating their words again and again . . . And when you fast, don't make it obvious, as the hypocrites do, for they try to look miserable and disheveled so people will admire them for their fasting. I tell you the truth; that is the only reward they will ever get. (Matt 6:7, 16)

If you want people to notice your piety, then go for it. Just understand that is all you are going to get. If, on the other hand, you seek the righteousness of God that comes by faith, then your reward will be such that even your very imagination will be overwhelmed.

The blessings of God are not given so that we can flaunt them. God's grace is meant to be shared with others, and our motivation for doing so is love. As Paul goes on to say, "For when we place our faith in Christ Jesus, there is no benefit in being circumcised or being uncircumcised . . . What is important is faith expressing itself in love" (Gal 5:6). Affirming that the rite of circumcision is irrelevant to the matter of ultimate righteousness, Paul reminds us that the true mark of faith is love. Without love, our faith easily turns into a harsh religiosity not unlike the ugly monster we know as legalism.

There are few things more disgusting than a person who claims to be a Christian yet behaves in a shamefully obnoxious manner. Knowing the truth of God is not a license to be rude. Unfortunately, there are many in my profession who miss this point entirely. A person saved by faith is in no position to boast about how well he or she believed. We can only declare, in all humility, how great God is to save. Furthermore, the blessings we receive should compel us to love others enough to share the gospel message with them. Evangelism is not a multilevel marketing strategy designed to bring in wealth. It is the loving act of showing people the way of salvation in order to see them live out the very same freedom we now enjoy as a result of the gracious work of Jesus Christ.

As a teenager, I worked as a theater usher for a few local gigs. I remember one particular concert in the early eighties. Our job was simple: as people entered the auditorium, we ushers were to seat them according to the color of their tickets. Those with gold tickets got to sit in the orchestra section, while those with red tickets had to sit up in the balcony. Unfortunately, a storm hit the city that night. The concert was not canceled, but a number of people never arrived. As a result, the auditorium was sparsely filled. When the concert began, the performer noticed that the few people who came were seated so far apart from each other. Not wanting to perform to such a thin crowd, he asked everyone, including those in the balcony, to move as close to the stage as possible. At this point, it didn't matter if audience members had a gold ticket or a red ticket; everyone got to enjoy the concert up close and personal, solely on the basis of the performer's invitation. The invitation of Christ is just like that. When Christ calls you to himself, it doesn't matter what is printed on your ticket—it only matters that you accept the invitation to be close to him. The love of Christ is so compelling that it doesn't make sense to reject it. It is a love so vast that there is enough for everyone to enjoy it fully.

Stay on Track

Many ancient philosophers used the imagery of a footrace to describe living a moral life. The elements of discipline, determination, fairness, single-mindedness, and finishing well all contribute to a nuanced understanding of what it means to live morally. Paul was also a fan of the footrace analogy. He even used it to describe his own life of faith (Phil 3:13–14; 2 Tim 4:7). However, there is a noticeable difference in Paul's use of the analogy. For Paul, the race was not based primarily on a runner's ability but on God's ability. We are only able to run faithfully because it is Christ who gives us the capacity to begin and complete the race. After all, he is "the champion who initiates and perfects our faith" (Heb 12:2).

In running the race of faith, the Galatians seem to have veered off-track. Paul says to them, "You were running the race so well . . . Who has held you back from following the truth?" (Gal 5:7). That they were once running well indicates that they had, in the past, put their faith in Christ upon hearing the gospel. But somehow, something was keeping them from following through with this commitment. Paul frames this in terms of someone holding them back. The term "held you back" literally means "cut you off." It's as if the Galatians were doing fine in the race until someone intending to keep them from completing the course deliberately got in their way.

During the 1984 Summer Olympic Games held in Los Angeles, a controversial race took place. American track star Mary Decker was a favorite to win the 3,000-meter race. Decker earned numerous gold medals throughout her career and even held over a dozen world records in various track events. But on that fateful summer day, the unimaginable happened. Decker was running in a tight pack when another runner, Zola Budd from South Africa, collided with her. Budd quickly recovered and continued to run. Decker, however, fell and badly injured her hip. Unable to continue the race, she watched in pain while Budd and the other runners completed the race. It remains uncertain if Zola Budd's action was deliberate or purely accidental. In any case, there is no doubt that she was the reason Decker was not able to finish the race. With all due respect to the South African Olympian, you and I need to be watchful of the spiritual Zola Budds in our lives.

One thing is certain: God is never the one responsible for holding you back from pursuing a fruitful life of faith. Responding to his own inquiry as to who was holding the Galatians back, Paul wrote, "It certainly isn't God, for he is the one who called you to freedom" (Gal 5:8). It's funny how we tend to blame our liberators. After Moses led the Hebrews out of Egypt, the people were extremely happy. But when they found themselves caught between the Red Sea and the armies of Pharaoh, they said to Moses,

> Why did you bring us out here to die in the wilderness? Weren't there enough graves for us in Egypt? What have you done to us? Why did you make us leave Egypt? Didn't we tell you this would happen while we were still in Egypt? We said, "Leave us alone! Let us be slaves to the Egyptians. It is better to be a slave in Egypt than a corpse in the wilderness!" (Exod 14:11–12)

If you think about it, they were not only blaming Moses. They were also blaming God, because it was he who told Moses to lead them out of Egypt. If we are honest with ourselves, we've probably done the same thing many times.

It is utterly foolish, however, to think that God, who gave us the blessing of righteousness and freedom, would suddenly turn against us and usurp the very freedom he gives. God was not the one getting in the way of the Galatian believers, the false teachers were! Their doctrines were like poison spreading around the church and infecting the believers with doubt. Paul aptly describes this threat by writing, "This false teaching is like a little yeast that spreads through the whole batch of dough!" (Gal 5:9). In the New Testament, yeast is often used as a symbol for sin. In his letter to the Corinthians, Paul said, "Your boasting about this is terrible. Don't you realize that this sin is like a little yeast that spreads through the whole batch of dough? Get rid of the old 'yeast' by removing this wicked person from among you. Then you will be a fresh batch of dough made without yeast, which is what you really are" (1 Cor 5:6–7). It seems there was someone in the Corinthian church who was living in sin, and unfortunately that sin was having a profound effect on the entire church. To deal with this matter, Paul insisted that the wicked person be removed from their presence. Likewise, this sinful yeast was also spreading throughout the Galatian church. Yet Paul remained confident that God would protect them. He said, "I am trusting the Lord to keep you from believing false teachings . . . God will judge that person, whoever he is, who has been confusing you" (Gal 5:10). Although sin is capable of spreading far and wide, the power of God is even more capable of triumphing over it. Confusing God's children with lies and deceptive teachings is a damnable offense. Jesus himself taught his disciples that "There will always be temptations to sin, but what sorrow awaits the person who does the tempting! . . . It would be better to be thrown into the sea with a millstone hung around your neck than to cause one of these little ones to fall into sin" (Luke 17:1–2). The judgment that awaits deceivers and false teachers is severe. It would be highly unwise for the Galatians to follow after the Judaizers, because their fate will be nothing less than the judgment of God.

Make Up Your Mind

It seems there were those in Galatia who accused Paul of teaching the same false doctrines being taught by the Judaizers. However, this would not sufficiently explain why Paul was being harassed by the false teachers themselves. He writes, "Dear brothers and sisters, if I were still preaching that you must be circumcised—as some say I do—why am I still being persecuted? . . . If I were no longer preaching salvation through the cross of Christ, no one would be offended" (Gal 5:11). Paul was pointing out inconsistencies in the accusations against him. If he was indeed teaching the same doctrine as the Judaizers, then there should have been no conflict between them. But in reality, the Judaizers were persecuting Paul precisely because his teachings were not in line with their deceptive gospel.

There's nothing like a good nemesis to clarify who we really are. Think about it. What is Superman without Lex Luthor, Spiderman without the Green Goblin, or Batman without the Joker? The position of our opponent can bring so much clarity to our own stance on an issue. Once each person's position is clear, others can make up their minds as to which side they are on. The Judaizers preached the way of the law, while Paul preached salvation through the cross of Christ. Paul's was not a popular gospel. In fact, he once said,

> The message of the cross is foolish to those who are headed for destruction! It is foolish to the Jews, who ask for signs from heaven. And it is foolishness to the Greeks, who seek human wisdom. So when we preach that Christ was crucified, the Jews are offended and the Gentiles say it's all nonsense. (1 Cor 1:18, 22–23)

How, then, could there have been any confusion that what Paul was preaching was identical to the preaching of the Judaizers? The two messages could not have been more different. The path of the cross is void of any human effort to be saved. It is utterly and completely the work of God through his Son, Jesus Christ.

Interestingly, we face a similar situation today. Modern societies are becoming more and more pluralistic as a large cross-section of people of various races and religions converge in the major cities of the world. In such a scenario, there is a temptation to treat all ideologies as equal so as not to risk offending anyone's sensibilities. So to say that Jesus is one of many ways to God is not a problem at all in a pluralistic society. However, to claim that Jesus is the *only* way to God threatens the concept of tolerance. And while the point of preaching the gospel is certainly not to offend anyone, it is virtually inevitable that some, if not many, will be offended by it anyway. But if we know the gospel to be the truth, we are compelled to tell it like it is. Of course, we must do so with gentleness and respect.

Because Paul loved the Galatians, he hated that they were exposed to such evil teachers. He said, "I just wish that those troublemakers who want to mutilate you by circumcision would mutilate themselves" (Gal 5:12). Again, Paul's use of wordplay is lucid. Sarcasm was, and continues to be, a skill common to good debaters. Winston Churchill was a master at it. When Lady Nancy Astor said to him, "Winston, if I were your wife, I'd poison your tea," he is said to have replied, "Nancy, if I was your husband,

I'd drink it." Paul, himself a master debater, also proved to be a quick wit. Carrying on the imagery of circumcision (which some viewed as a form of mutilation), he longed to see the Judaizers cut off from the community in Galatia. Paul was not wishing for their death, only their removal. That way, they would cease having such a negative influence on the lives of the Galatian believers.

It was up to the Galatians to choose which side to believe. Should they side with Paul and continue in the path of faith, or should they side with the Judaizers and revert to the way of the law? They had to make up their mind one way or another, lest they become like the boy who could not tell his tailor if he wanted shorts or trousers. When the boy came to the shop to pick up his order, he was horrified to see that the tailor had made one leg short and the other long. It was then that the boy decided never again to let someone else make his decisions for him. There's a lesson in there for all of us. If you decide not to decide, you can be sure somebody else will decide for us. In matters of faith and salvation, these are decisions you do not want to hand over to someone else.

Choose Wisely

Each believer is a free being and therefore has the ability to use that freedom to make choices. It is important, however, to understand that not all choices are created equal. Paul said to the Galatians, "For you have been called to live in freedom, my brothers and sisters . . . But don't use your freedom to satisfy your sinful nature . . . Instead, use your freedom to serve one another in love" (Gal 5:13). It would be easy for an immature believer to conclude that since he or she is now free, everything permissible is also good. Not so. When faced with choices, we must be mature enough to recognize that there is a world of difference between good choices and bad choices. Or as Paul put it, "I am allowed to do anything—but not everything is beneficial" (1 Cor 10:23). What a truism! In a country like America, for instance, you are free to smoke cigarettes (in designated areas), but that does not mean smoking is good for you. You and another person can have consensual sex, yet doing so may soon prove damaging to your other relationships. Freedom to do something does not mean that something is a good thing. It only means that, in a free environment, you should be willing to live with the consequences of your choices. If you are promiscuous, then don't complain if you contract a disease. If you like climbing trees, don't whine when you fall and break an arm. Consequences are all part of the deal.

To approach it philosophically, freedom is not simply the liberty to do whatever we wish (which is more akin to anarchy); rather, freedom is being empowered and enabled to do what is right. When a prisoner is released on parole, he is not set free to commit more crimes, for more misdeeds will only land him back in prison. Instead, this freedom is an opportunity to finally do what he should have been doing in the first place—live an honorable life free from crime. The sinner who is redeemed by Christ and freed by grace is not liberated to go on sinning. When Jesus forgave the adulterous woman, he said to her, "Go and sin no more" (John 8:11). You are free to make your own choices, but just be sure they are good choices.

What constitutes a good choice? For starters, Paul told the Galatians to "serve one another in love." What better way to counter our selfish tendencies than to reach out lovingly to those in need? Ironically, "serving" is sometimes used as a reference to slavery. Paul asserts that we are no longer slaves to the law but that as free people, we can willingly enslave ourselves for a good cause. This is a unique brand of slavery because it is born out of a free will and a transformed heart.

Paul continues to explain, "For the whole law can be summed up in this one command: 'Love your neighbor as yourself' . . . But if you are always biting and devouring one another, watch out! . . . Beware of destroying one another" (Gal 5:14–15). This statement, directed to the Judaizers and their sympathizers, is a reminder that the law is ultimately not about rules but about love. Unfortunately, many religionists miss this crucial point. We normally associate the command to love our neighbor with the teachings of Christ, yet we forget that this was part of the original law given to Moses (Lev 19:18). Loving your neighbor is not just a New Testament principle, it is also a biblical principle. Even if this command was written within the context of the law, it is a code that supersedes legalism in that even free believers are invited to behave according to its precepts. Failure to choose the way of love leads to a sort of religious cannibalism in which we end up "biting and devouring one another." True freedom leads to a life of edification, not destruction.

In Lewis Carroll's *Alice's Adventures in Wonderland*, an interesting conversation takes place between Alice and the Cheshire Cat. Alice is walking along a path when she happens upon the Cat. She asks, "Would you tell me, please, which way I ought to go from here?" The Cat answers,

"That depends a good deal on where you want to get to." "I don't much care where," Alice replies. "Then it doesn't matter which way you go," advises the Cat.

What a brilliant response! If you don't know where you want to go, it doesn't matter which path you take. But Christians know where to go; therefore, it matters which road we take. There is a road that leads to spiritual imprisonment and one that leads to eternal joy with Christ. You are free to choose, so choose wisely.

11

Adding Fruit to Your Diet

Galatians 5:16–26

HAVE YOU EVER WONDERED what humans first ate? I don't know the scientific answer, but according to Scripture, humans were originally vegan. After God created man and woman, God said to them, "Look! I have given you every seed-bearing plant throughout the earth and all the fruit trees for your food" (Gen 1:29). Coincidentally, the same diet was offered to the rest of the animal kingdom as well. Can you imagine a lion munching on broccoli for lunch and a nice juicy peach for dessert? While the food chain has since expanded to include animals, there is still something to be said for the foundational role of vegetation in cuisine. I am not a vegan (not yet, at least), but I have a lot of respect for people who are.

The benefits of a vegan diet have been extolled for ages. Even the Bible reminds us that Daniel turned out to be more fit than his contemporaries when he refused the king's rich foods and stuck to a diet of fruit, vegetables, and water. Conversely, diets in which vegetables are minimal or altogether absent have demonstrably adverse effects on the human body. The United States Department of Agriculture recommends we consume at least two to four servings of fruit each day. Fruit is a great source of vitamins and fiber, aids the digestive process, and helps lower cholesterol levels. Adding fruit to our diets simply makes good nutritional sense.

Our spiritual lives also involve fruit—but a different kind of fruit. You see, we who live by the Holy Spirit are expected to produce spiritual fruit. Fruit is often a biblical euphemism for behavior. It represents an observable manifestation of things unseen. As Jesus once said to his disciples,

> Beware of false prophets who come disguised as harmless sheep but are really wolves. You can identify them by their fruit, that is, by the way they act. Can you pick grapes from thornbushes, or figs from thistles? A good tree produces good fruit, and a bad tree produces bad fruit. A good tree can't produce bad fruit, and a bad tree can't produce good fruit. So every tree that does not produce

> good fruit is chopped down and thrown into the fire. Yes, just as you can identify a tree by its fruit, so you can identify people by their actions. (Matt 7:15–20)

The Apostle Paul was clearly familiar with this teaching. In fact, Paul picks up from where Jesus leaves off and applies the principle of fruit-bearing to the situation in Galatia. Just as Jesus taught that people can be known by their fruit, the false teachers in Galatia could be exposed as frauds simply by taking the time to examine their fruit—that is, their habitual behaviors. And since this portion of Paul's letter contains practical advice for Christian living, Paul also takes time to let believers know how they ought to behave in contrast to the Judaizers' misguided actions.

The Battle Within

Paul ended the previous part of his letter by telling the Galatians not to do anything that would destroy each other. Now he offers an alternative to such destructive behavior. Paul writes, "So I say, let the Holy Spirit guide your lives . . . Then you won't be doing what your sinful nature craves" (Gal 5:16). Indeed, the best way to keep from living in sin is to live by the Spirit. In the King James Version of the Bible, the phrase "let the Holy Spirit guide you" is rendered as "walk in the Spirit." Ancient writers commonly used walking as a poetic way of describing a pattern of behavior. It's as if Paul was saying, "Behave spiritually." In this case, the spiritual is pitted against the carnal.

In the New Testament, two words are used to contrast the two dimensions of human nature—*pneuma* and *sarx*. *Pneuma*, from the Greek word for "breath" and "air," refers to the spirit. With reference to God, it is usually qualified as the *Sacred Pneuma*, or Holy Spirit. The spirit is associated with the inner person—the real you. Sometimes used interchangeably with the term "soul," spirit is the life element that governs a person's thought, emotion, and volition. It is in our spirit that we truly encounter God. In this sense, God's Spirit encounters our spirit.

Sarx, on the other hand, refers to the flesh. Literally, the flesh describes the person's physical dimension, or the body. In the flesh we are able to interact with the physical world through the use of our five senses. However, when Paul uses the word "flesh," he is talking about something more substantial than our physical bodies. Flesh also represents human works and efforts—qualities of a carnal mindset. Carnality (a term from where we also get the word "meat") is essentially the expression of our sinful nature. When we are carnal, we are living according to our sinful drives rather than by the leading of the Spirit. Interestingly, Paul links carnality to the way of the law because, unlike the way of the promise, it is fueled by human effort rather than by the filling of the Holy Spirit.

Have you ever been in a car that ran out of gas? I'm old enough to remember the oil crisis of 1973, when the oil-producing nations in the Middle East cut supplies to the United States and its allies. I was living in Manila then, which was affected by the embargo. For days, perhaps weeks, our family car—a green Hillman Hunter—just sat in the garage, completely immobile. It could not run without fuel. Then word got out that gasoline was finally available. But how were we to get the car from the house to the gas station? We had no other choice. My mom took the wheel of the car while my dad, my brother, and I pushed the car all the way to the local Shell station a few miles from home. The car was moving not because it was powered with gasoline but because we were pushing it with our own strength. That image reminds me of how some people live. Void of any spiritual power, they strive to live on their own strength each day. But our carnal strength is no match for the demands of life. Without spiritual fuel, we live substandard lives and succumb to our sinful passions because they seem the easiest path to take. Think about it—without fuel, a car moves fastest only when going downhill.

We need to live by the Spirit because only the Holy Spirit can keep us on the path to freedom. It is not enough to be free; it is also important to *stay* free. In the film *The Next Three Days*, John Brennan (played by Russell Crowe) is faced with a future without his wife because she was serving a life sentence for murder. He is convinced she is innocent, but all legal options have been exhausted. He determines that his wife's only hope for freedom is for him to help her escape from prison. John consults with Damon Pennington (played by Liam Neeson), an ex-convict who successfully escaped from prison seven times. Out of curiosity, John asks Damon why it was seven times. Damon replies, "Escaping is easy, the hardest part is staying free." So true, isn't it? And I imagine the same is true in the spiritual realm. It is one thing to be set free to enjoy the promise of God's eternal blessings. It is quite another to remain free amidst countless obstacles and distractions. Our only hope of sustaining the wonderful gift of liberty in Christ is to walk in the Spirit.

Fooling Ourselves with Fig Leaves

Paul was mindful that believers face many challenges to faith. He said to the Galatians, "The sinful nature wants to do evil, which is just the opposite of what the Spirit wants . . . And the Spirit gives us desires that are the opposite of what the sinful nature desires . . . These two forces are constantly fighting each other, so you are not free to carry out your good intentions" (Gal 5:17). A battle takes place in the heart of each believer. In one corner is the flesh that entices us to feed the desires of our sinful nature. In the other corner is the Spirit, who leads us to do only what is good. Flesh and Spirit are at opposite ends of the spectrum. In the original text, Paul says they contend "against" each other.

The Apostle Paul was himself no stranger to this battle. In his letter to the Romans, Paul confessed,

> So the trouble is not with the law, for it is spiritual and good. The trouble is with me, for I am all too human, a slave to sin. I don't really understand myself, for I want to do what is right, but I don't do it. Instead, I do what I hate. But if I know that what I am doing is wrong, this shows that I agree that the law is good. So I am not the one doing wrong; it is sin living in me that does it. And I know that nothing good lives in me, that is, in my sinful nature. I want to do what is right, but I can't. I want to do what is good, but I don't. I don't want to do what is wrong, but I do it anyway. But if I do what I don't want to do, I am not really the one doing wrong; it is sin living in me that does it. (Rom 7:14-20)

That is a bit difficult to read, isn't it? For a moment, it seemed like Paul was about to break out a tongue twister. But the assertion is quite serious. The battle within us is such that the two opposing forces of flesh and Spirit cause a degree of inner conflict that is difficult to explain. There is the good we want to do, yet there is also the impulse to do what we should not do.

The good news, of course, is that we do not face this battle alone. That is why we are given the gift of the Holy Spirit. As a believer matures in faith, he or she learns to surrender his or her will to the leading of the Spirit. It takes patience to reach this level because maturity is a process—and a life-long process at that. Fortunately, once we start yielding to the Holy Spirit, we are already, and immediately, released from our bondage to the law. As Paul declared, "But when you are directed by the Spirit, you are not under obligation to the law of Moses" (Gal 5:18).

People who are led by the Spirit have the advantage of not having to second-guess the thoughts of God. As a young seminarian, I took an advanced class in New Testament Studies. The professor happened to have authored one of the required textbooks for the class. The book was rather dense and highly technical. Not only was the text linguistically challenging, it was also philosophically exigent. Late one evening, feeling unable to struggle through the material any longer, I decided to call it a night and just deal with it the next day. The following morning on my way to the classroom, I noticed the lights in my professor's office were on. Since I was on campus early, I figured I would go ahead and visit his office to ask him about the contents of his book, which I found most difficult to understand. Graciously, he let me in, sat me down, and started to explain all the parts of the book I had assumed I was too dumb to understand. With every minute of his masterful explanation, things got clearer. The mysteries seemed less mysterious, and my mind seemed better able to grasp the course material. What an advantage to have personal access to the author of a book! Even better, how wonderful that we who read the Bible with an attitude of faith gain access to the author of those words—the Holy Spirit himself. In seeking the mind of God, we are no longer dependent on the letter of the law because of the personal relationship we have with God.

Worst-case Scenario

What about those who do not live by the Spirit? Who do they follow in their religious pursuits? Unfortunately, those of a reprobate mind succumb to the provocations of the flesh. Paul explains the consequences of this way of life:

> When you follow the desires of your sinful nature, the results are very clear: sexual immorality, impurity, lustful pleasures, idolatry, sorcery, hostility, quarreling, jealousy, outbursts of anger, selfish ambition, dissension, division, envy, drunkenness, wild parties, and other sins like these. (Gal 5:19–21)

In this section, Paul begins to demonstrate the difference between walking in the Spirit and living by the flesh. He does so by creating lists. In the ancient world, it was common for moralists to employ lists that served as guidelines for moral living. Paul's lists were no different. As guidelines, they are not exhaustive collections of every conceivable sin. Nor is there any suggestion that every sinner is fully capable of committing each of the sins listed. These guidelines simply offer an ample array of behaviors that paint an accurate picture of what carnal living looks like. Paul's list also provides the Galatians with practical instructions on how to spot a false teacher. As an enumeration of the obvious and unsavory results of sinfulness, the items on Paul's list fall under four general categories: sensual iniquities, religious perversions, social transgressions, and pagan behavior.

Paul begins with sexual iniquities because these are almost universally viewed as the most obvious manifestations of sin. First is "sexual immorality," a term that generally covers any number of sexual relationships outside the blessing of marriage. Paul, in fact, uses the term *porneia*, which is where we get English words such as "fornication" and "pornography." "Impurity" can refer to a person who engages in behavior that is either morally or ceremonially unclean. Ceremonial uncleanness was a particular concern to Judaizers because of the many rules surrounding this issue found in the Torah. "Lustful pleasures" comes from a term that means "licentiousness" or "unrestrained sexuality." It refers to people who flaunt their sexual exploits with no sense of shame. Such vulgarities are expressed both in words and in deeds. You would think Paul had a vision of the present world when he came up with this list, but surprisingly, it was a description of the world in which he lived. It is a reminder that sexual iniquity in not a modern phenomenon but an ancient one, and even the believers of yesteryear had to be mindful of such temptations.

The second category, religious perversions, includes two specific sins. The first is "idolatry." This sin, perhaps one of the most ancient, refers to any act in which creation, rather than the Creator, is given worship and praise. In the Torah, idolatry is a violation of the first two commandments found in the Decalogue. Idolatry was a rampant practice among the pagans in Galatia, and the believers there would have been well aware of what Paul was talking about. Idols can come in many forms, but they were commonly actual physical objects. Idols were often images of people or creatures carved from wood or forged out of metal. But there is more to idolatry than just bowing before a graven image. Non-physical idols exist as well. Anything we worship other than God is an idol. Such idols can include wealth, power, other individuals, and even oneself. The evil of idolatry is that it robs individuals of living out their primary purpose, which is to love the Lord supremely and primarily (Matt 22:37). The second religious perversion is simply called "sorcery." In modern times, sorcery is associated with fairy tales and medieval folklore. But the biblical term used by Paul takes a somewhat different angle. In the original text, the word "sorcery" is actually the term *pharmakeia*. It is where we get the modern word "pharmacy." It turns out that some ancient sorcery practices were accompanied by the use of chemical substances or poisons. In modern times, we would call them drugs. Although the practice of medieval sorcery is no longer common in the modern world (at least not in the Western world), the use of drugs is still prevalent. Indeed, drugs such as hallucinogens and psychedelics are often used to alter perception in hopes of achieving a "religious" experience of some sort. That is not to say that modern drug use parallels the ancient practices of sorcery, but some of the similarities are certainly uncanny.

The third category is a list of social transgressions. These are sins we commit against other people (and this category makes up, perhaps intentionally, the longest list of the four). Paul begins with "hostility." In other versions of the Bible, the word used is "hatred." In many cases, this involves hateful behavior toward another person or group because of what makes them different—such as matters of race, religion, physical appearance, ideology, or creed. This can lead to "quarreling." Beyond the typical squabbles common among siblings, quarreling is the kind of strife and discord that results from hostility. Because we hate what is different about another person, we quarrel with them and, consequently, the gap between us becomes even wider. To put it another way, quarreling is born out of failure on our part to find common ground with others. When I was in seminary, one of my closest friends was a gentleman who attended a neighboring university—and he happened to be a Muslim. Every Friday, we and a few friends would meet up for dinner, watch a movie, or even stay home for a game of checkers. Although there was a world of difference in our theological views, we found enough similarities between us that we did not have to resort to hostility or quarreling.

The third in this list is "jealousy." In the Bible, jealousy actually has positive and negative dimensions. For instance, God is sometimes depicted as a jealous God. But we are not to assign to God the same kind of jealousy a teenage boy feels when the girl he likes flirts with another boy. God's is a righteous jealousy in which he is pained by our failure to recognize authentic worship and settle instead for cheap imitations. In contrast, the kind of jealousy Paul talks about is being upset that you do not have what someone else has, or wishing nobody else will be allowed to enjoy something you cannot have. I'm reminded of the story of a man who finds a bottle on the ground. He rubs it, and out comes a genie. The genie says, "I'm old and tired, so I'm only going to grant you one wish; however, be advised that whatever I give you, your worst enemy in life will get double what you ask for." The man thought long and hard and finally said, "Make me blind in one eye!" Now *that's* jealousy!

Then there is "outbursts of anger." Again, just like jealousy, anger is a normal human response. In fact, there are times when anger is the right response to a given situation. But this kind of anger is difficult to practice. As Aristotle observed, "Anyone can become angry—that is easy . . . but to be angry with . . . the right person at the right time, and for the right purpose, and in the right way—this is not within everybody's power and is not easy."[1] The anger of God is also known as righteous indignation, but the anger Paul speaks of is an indignation brought about by hatred and jealousy. It is characterized by uncontrolled emotional outbursts of volcanic proportions. The result of this kind of anger is bitterness, dissension, and, ironically, even more anger. Sometimes such anger takes over your cognitive faculties to the point that you don't even know why you are angry—you just know that you are. Any number of unpleasant consequences can be the unfortunate result of such anger.

Anger is followed by "selfish ambition," which comes from the word for "contention." "Selfish ambition" refers to a self-centered approach to doing things—that is, failing to take others into consideration. Few things irritate me more than inconsiderate people. On a smaller scale, I see it all the time when I go grocery shopping. Inevitably, a person in front of me will stop, leave his or her cart in the middle of the aisle, and walk away to browse for some hard-to-find product. Meanwhile, I'm stuck between that cart and other shoppers around me, all because this person failed to consider how his or her actions would affect me. Pretty selfish, don't you think? But this self-centered thinking affects more serious matters than mere grocery shopping. Whether it happens at home, at the office, or even in recreation, some people tend to think of only themselves when making plans.

The next two sins, "dissention" and "division," are closely related, except that they each emphasize a unique characteristic of disunity. On the one hand, dissention has to do with being a disagreeable person—someone who never seems to take time to see another point of view. This is clearly one of the results of selfish ambition. In fact, the very word "division" literally means "two visions," or seeing things in a way that is different from another. For some, it's always "My way or the highway." Paul's use of the

---

1. Aristotle, *Nicomachean Ethics*, trans. H. Rackham (Harvard University Press, 1934) 111.

term "division" likely refers more to sectarianism or feuds. It can be understood as the natural result of dissention. If you never take the time to understand where others are coming from, it only makes sense that you and they will become enemies. In time, you and the other party may attract sympathizers as others take sides, resulting in an unmanageable all-out feud. The Hatfield-McCoy feud of the 1880s, for example, resulted in bitterness, deaths, lawsuits, libelous accusations, and disastrous consequences that spanned multiple generations in what must truly be one of the saddest historical commentaries on relationships gone wrong.

The last social transgression is "envy." This is very similar to jealousy, but whereas jealousy involves feeling spiteful toward what others have, envy has more to do with craving what others have, especially when you shouldn't (or couldn't) have it in the first place. The Ten Commandments calls this "coveting" and specifically lists things that should not be taken unlawfully: "You must not covet your neighbor's house . . . You must not covet your neighbor's wife, male or female servant, ox or donkey, or anything else that belongs to your neighbor" (Exod 20:17). Envy is a highly deceptive sin because those who are caught in it are led to believe they cannot get satisfaction without of having what someone else has. Envy is the antithesis of contentment. When we covet our neighbor's house, we forget that our own dwelling has already been provided by God. Yet, instead of being thankful for our living situation, we crave someone else's mansion. Those who are habitually envious continue to slide down an unending spiral of discontentment, and it is indeed a sad sight to see a person go mad craving things he or she may already have. Furthermore, that we don't have certain things might actually be a blessing from God. God knows what we need and what we don't need, just like a good parent. Ana and I don't give our kids everything they ask for, but that doesn't make us bad parents. In fact, it likely means we are doing a great job as parents. If our kids continue to sulk over what they do not get, they become the only true losers. In the spiritual realm, the same principle holds true.

The final category, pagan behavior, includes two sins. First is "drunkenness." This does not simply refer to consumption of alcoholic beverages. For that matter, it is not even limited to the use of alcohol alone, although in Paul's letter, that would be the primary implication. "Drunkenness" refers to the overconsumption of alcohol (or similar substances) in such a way as to dull thinking and hinder good judgment. When people are drunk, they tend to say and do things they regret once sober. For some reason, drunkenness removes the filter that prevents us from saying or doing inappropriate things. Sometimes this inhibition can have positive results, such as in the case of the man who did not stutter as long as he was drunk. But this is a rarity. For the most part, the results of drunkenness are less than desirable and at times even deadly. The second kind of pagan behavior, "wild parties," is usually connected with drunkenness. Ancient pagan parties were marked by extensive use of alcohol, gluttonous feasting, and sexual orgies. If that sounds too much like the kind of parties you attend, take heed. The object of this warning is not to prevent you from having fun but rather to provoke reflection on how much fun those parties ultimately are. In the long run, hangovers are not fun. Neither is weight gain from overeating. And how about sexually transmitted diseases or unwanted pregnancies? Am I saying that all of these consequences are sure to happen to you? Of course not. I know people who have lived this way for years and seem to still be enjoying it scot-free. But remember, we are talking long-term consequences—even when the short-term effects might actually be pleasurable.

Paul pulls no punches in disclosing the ultimate long-term consequence for following our sinful desires. He wrote, "Let me tell you again, as I have before, that anyone living that sort of life will not inherit the Kingdom of God" (Gal 5:21). As you can see, a false teacher is not simply one who gives wrong instructions, but also one who lives immorally. Without the salvific blessing of Christ, such a person is bound to spend an eternity outside the presence of God, void of any inheritance that would otherwise be available through his grace. And if the path of sin leads toward that direction, it certainly doesn't make sense for any of us to follow suit. The path of righteousness is the only one that makes good sense.

Ripe for Harvest

It is never enough to tell people what not to do. The "Say No to Drugs" campaign, for instance, is only useful if drug addicts are told what to say *yes* to. Otherwise, he or she might just give up one drug for another. Likewise, giving believers a list of behaviors that ought to be avoided is helpful but incomplete. By itself, the list still leaves us wondering what must be done instead. Theology must precede ethics, but it cannot be good theology until it is applied ethically. After we determine what to believe, we still must ask an important question—that is, in the words of Francis Schaeffer, "How should we then live?"[2] It's a gracious way of saying, "So what?"

Paul does not hesitate to address the matter of proper Christian behavior. Interestingly, he frames it not in terms of actions to perform but rather in terms of qualities to possess. He said, "But the Holy Spirit produces this kind of fruit in our lives: love, joy peace, patience, kindness, goodness, faithfulness, gentleness, and self-control" (Gal 5:22–23). Two things are immediately obvious at this point. First, Paul refers to the "fruit" of the Spirit even though he just spoke about the "works" of the flesh. You would think Paul would compare carnal *works* with spiritual *works*, yet instead, he speaks of *fruit*. The reason for this wordplay is quite apparent. Whereas sinful behavior is the product of our doing, having Christ-like qualities is a product of our being. That is, being joined to Christ just as a branch is joined to a tree trunk, the believer will produce fruit naturally—and yes, effortlessly. Jesus actually preached a sermon on this. He said, "Yes, I am the vine; you are the branches . . . Those who remain in me, and I in them, will produce much fruit . . . For apart from me you can do nothing" (John 15:5). Notice how Jesus does not command us to produce fruit; he simply invites us to be joined to him. Fruit-bearing is the inevitable outcome of abiding in Christ.

The second observation is that Paul uses the singular term "fruit" as opposed to the plural "fruits." I believe this was intentional. The workings of the Holy Spirit in our lives are to be taken as a collective whole rather than as items in a spiritual smorgasbord. The fruit of the Spirit is more like a bunch of grapes. Each grape in an independent edible fruit, but each exists among other grapes as integral parts of a single unit.

This passage actually lends itself to a few more observations that may be less obvious but strongly implied. First, it takes time for fruit to ripen. The enemy of enjoying good fruit is impatience. In a recent Smucker's commercial, two boys are looking at some fruit hanging from a tree. One boy wants to take the fruit, but the other boy tells him to wait because the best way to enjoy the fruit is to pick it at the right time. The qualities described by the fruit of the Spirit take time to ripen in our lives. We are never perfectly loving, or kind, or gentle. But as long as we abide in Christ, we will continue to develop these qualities as the Spirit works in us. Second, fruit is intended to benefit others, not itself. A mango tree does not consume

---

2. See Francis Schaeffer, *How Should We Then Live? The Rise and Decline of Western Thought and Culture* (Wheaton, IL: Crossway, 2005).

mangoes, nor does a grapevine drink its own wine. When the Spirit produces fruit in us, it is primarily for the benefit of those around us. Our love is meant for the unloved, our kindness is for those who need help, and our patience is for those who need just a little more time to grow up. Finally, fruit is an accurate basis for identification. When we moved to our new home, one of the first things I noticed was a tree just outside the dining room window. I asked my wife, "What kind of tree is that?" "I don't know," she answered. It's been about six years, and I still don't know what kind of tree it is. Recently, I visited a friend's house. When I looked out toward his backyard, I said, "Hey, you have a lemon tree!" How did I know that? I can't identify the tree in my own backyard, but I immediately knew what kind of tree my friend had. It was simple really. His tree had fruit, while mine had none. That made all the difference in the world. When people see you, is the fruit of the Spirit so evident in your life that it leaves no doubt as to who you are in Christ? I certainly hope so.

The nine qualities that make up the fruit of the Spirit listed in Galatians can be broken down into three categories. There are three *upward* qualities that describe our relationship with God, there are three *outward* qualities that describe our relationship with others, and there are three *inward* qualities that describe our relationship with ourselves.

The first upward quality is "love." Although the English word "love" tends to be taken as a generic, all-encompassing term, there are actually many New Testament terms for love. For instance, *eros* is a sensual or romantic kind of love, while *phileo* is friendship or brotherly love, and *storge* is love between family members. Paul, however, uses the term *agape*. *Agape* is difficult to describe linguistically because it is rarely found in classical literature. It turns out, *agape* appears most often in the biblical text, and it has therefore come to mean the love of God. It is often described further as the unconditional love of God. So as you can see, Paul could not have chosen a more perfect word to describe the first of the nine spiritual qualities. Some have even argued that love is the foundation for the other eight. A believer is able to love unconditionally only because he or she has been loved unconditionally. Those who have never experienced the love of God will find it impossible to express this kind of love to others.

The second quality is "joy." While joy might be understood as happiness, it actually runs much deeper than that. Happiness is a feeble emotion that depends on favorable circumstances. Unfortunately, happiness can disappear without any advanced notice. When I'm told I just won a million dollars, I immediately become happy; when I'm told it was just a joke, I immediately feel unhappy. Easy come, easy go. Joy, on the other hand, is not an emotion but an attitude. Rather than depending on circumstances, joy rests on the person and nature of God, and God is unchanging. Joy does not mean we are constantly laughing or smiling. It *does* mean we are so at rest in the presence of God that even the most trying circumstance cannot shake us.

The third quality is "peace." This is such a common term today, but I'm afraid many of us fail to appreciate the depth of its meaning. The modern understanding of peace tends to be the mere absence of conflict. Yet the absence of conflict can be attributed to circumstances other than peace. For instance, during the Cold War, no actual battles were fought between the United States and the Soviet Union. It would be wrong, however, to conclude that both countries were at peace with each other. In this case, it was not peace but the balance of power that created a semblance of tranquility. No one pulled the trigger only because each side knew the other could just as easily fire back.

The biblical notion of peace runs much deeper. Based on the Old Testament concept of *shalom*, peace is possessing inner tranquility even in the midst of conflict and turmoil. It is inner wholeness that allows us to deal with external strife. Imagine an airplane cruising at 35,000 feet. Normally, the air pressure at that altitude would be such that the plane's fuselage would be crushed. But why does it remain intact? The answer is cabin pressure. Because the airplane is pressurized from within, it is able to counter the external pressure. As a result, the plane is at peace, so to speak. Life is so full of external pressures and conflict that only the Holy Spirit can pressurize us with the peace of God from within. This allows us to remain tranquil no matter what circumstance we face.

The second category, the outward qualities, affects our relationships with the people around us. It begins with "patience." Patience is sometimes associated with endurance. In the Bible, however, "endurance" is normally used in the context of facing tribulations, while "patience" is used in the context of being tolerant of people. In other words, even when we endure hard times, we are patient with others. In fact, the term Paul used is better translated as "long-suffering." I've always said that praying for patience is one of the most dangerous things you can ask of God, because the only way for God to answer that prayer is to bring a trying circumstance or annoying person into your life. After all, how else do you expect to practice patience?

Fooling Ourselves with Fig Leaves

With the help of the Holy Spirit, you can exercise patience beyond your normal capacity to put up with all kinds of people.

Secondly, there is "kindness." This refers to our ability to perform considerate acts toward others, especially when they do not necessarily deserve to be treated kindly. It is being gracious toward others in the same way God has been gracious toward us. Remember how Jesus taught us to be kind to our enemies? We are told to love them and pray for their happiness. How can we ever do such a thing? Only by the power of the Holy Spirit.

The third quality is "goodness." Goodness is linked to the concept of generosity. I've heard it said that you can give without loving, but you can't love without giving. The trait of goodness expresses itself in showing extravagant benevolence toward those in need. Goodness is the natural outcome of kindness. The Spirit of God causes us to be sensitive to the material and spiritual poverty that surrounds us each day. This compels us to do what we can to alleviate the pain of those we encounter in the course of our lives. Practically everyone I know desires to be a good person, but only God, who is perfectly good, can make us truly good.

Finally, there is the third category—the inward qualities. These are qualities that are born and bred in our innermost being. First is "faithfulness." This means we are trustworthy and reliable. Faithful people are true to their word, and they keep their promises even when it is difficult to do so. Jesus told many parables about faithfulness. In the parable of the talents (Luke 19:11–27), for instance, even those who are faithful with few things are entrusted with great things.

The second inward quality is "gentleness." The term used by Paul also means "meekness," "humility," and "lowliness." In modern thought, meekness is viewed as weakness. But nothing could be further from the truth. In fact, it takes a lot of strength to be gentle. A good way to think of gentleness is strength under control. Imagine a large man who is able to break bricks with his bare hands. Isn't it fascinating that this same man can carry his infant daughter with such tender care? He is not any weaker when carrying his daughter; rather, he is simply using the same strength with a good dose of control. Gentle people are not harsh in dealing with others. This fruit is the opposite of "rage" or "anger," which are works of the flesh.

Last, but not least, is "self-control." This means living with such self-restraint that we are able to overcome our tendency toward evil and sinful behavior. In everyday life, we think of having self-control when doing things like dieting or even dating. These are certainly within the umbrella of self-restraint, but the spiritual fruit of self-control is much heftier than that. Self-control is illustrated by a person who, even while walking through a dirty environment, nevertheless manages to keep clean. Whenever I cook, my clothes get awfully messy. That's why I admire chefs who keep their pearly white jackets clean even while preparing an elaborate meal. Their mastery over cooking tools and ingredients demonstrate such control that no matter how chaotic things get in the kitchen, they themselves remain unstained. That's the kind of self-control a Christian exercises in a world filled with the works of the flesh.

There you have it, the fruit of the Spirit—nine qualities that mark a person who lives by faith. But what guidelines or stipulations help us govern these fruit? None are needed. Regarding spiritual fruit, Paul wrote, "There is no law against these things!" (Gal 5:23). This is a rhetorical statement against the Judaizers, who are so obsessed over rules and regulations that they totally miss out on living out the spirit of the law they so love. There is no need for laws to monitor or restrict the fruit of the Spirit because the qualities of spiritual living are in complete harmony with what the laws of God have always been about. The law is useful in making us aware of the holiness of God, but only the Holy Spirit can cause us to live in a way that reflects his glory.

Crucifying the Flesh

Throughout my childhood, I was surrounded by images of the crucified Christ. This type of relic is known as a crucifix—a representation of the cross with an image of Christ on it. You've seen them in virtually every horror movie. As the vampires and demons attack, some priest comes in holding a crucifix in one hand and a prayer book in the other. As the priest raises the crucifix toward the demon, the evil spirits shudder in fear and flee for their lives. Meanwhile, back in the real world, a different kind of crucifixion is called for. Paul said to the Galatian believers, "Those who belong to Christ Jesus have nailed the passions and desires of their sinful nature to his cross and crucified them there" (Gal 5:24). Crucifixion was a brutal form of capital punishment under the Roman Empire. A criminal was fastened to a wooden cross by nails thrust through the hands and feet. The criminal was then left to hang there to die a slow but sure death. For a person who chooses to live by the Spirit, the only hope of overcoming the works of the flesh is to crucify ungodly appetites. That's exactly what happened when Christ was crucified. The Bible says, "For God made Christ, who never sinned, to be the offering for our sin, so that we could be made right with God through Christ" (2 Cor 5:21). When we crucify our sinful desires, we no longer need to concern ourselves with carnal passions. Having identified ourselves with the crucified Christ, we choose to relinquish our affinity with sinfulness at once, so much so that our earthly passions are rendered captive to the salvific work of Jesus Christ on the cross—our sins are crucified with him. This does not mean that we will no longer struggle with the temptation to sin but rather that the Holy Spirit is with us as we face daily struggles.

Our sinful desires die a slow death but a sure one. Much as a convicted criminal dies when given a lethal injection, death may not be immediate but it is inevitable. We may not appear to be immediately freed from the stronghold of sin, but in Christ, we are free indeed. And so Paul is able to say, "Since we are living by the Spirit, let us follow the Spirit's leading in every part of our lives" (Gal 5:25). Having reached a point of no return, we should not even entertain the thought of returning to our old way of life. Instead, we are to fully commit ourselves to living the way Christ wants us to live. Have you ever tried jumping over a chasm only to hesitate as you begin to leap? You are surely going to fall. The only way to make it to the other side is to run and jump with such reckless abandon that you don't even consider doing anything else.

In closing this section, Paul writes, "Let us not become conceited, or provoke one another, or be jealous of one another" (Gal 5:26). This warning comes at the heels of contrasting the works of the flesh and the fruit of the Spirit. We are spiritual people; therefore, we must live in the Spirit. There is no room in our hearts for vanity, disunity, or envy, so let's not even try to stuff those temptations in. There's nothing like keeping our hearts healthy with a hefty serving of spiritual fruit.

12

Reap It Good

Galatians 6:1–10

I'M NOT A FARMER, but I enjoy living next to a farm. Each day as I drive by it on my way to work, I notice how farmers always seem to be busy working. It appears the life of a farmer includes very little idle time. I'm especially fascinated by how farmers function as both artists and scientists. As artists, they have the field as their canvas and use seeds as their medium. In time, their once dull brown fields are blanketed by a vast array of crops that look so vibrant, you would think Michelangelo himself painted a masterpiece on the tilled soil. But at the same time, farmers operate according to very precise scientific principles. Everything from soil preparation to seed selection and even keeping track of the proper time for plowing, planting, and harvesting play an integral role in producing healthy crop. One particular principle that farmers must master is that of "sowing and reaping."

The farming industry thrives on understanding the dynamics of planting and harvesting. If a farmer fails to abide by this principle, the results will certainly be disastrous. If they plant at the wrong time, if they sow the wrong seeds, if they fail to water their crop, or if they harvest too early, things can easily go awry. In the spiritual world, the same principle of sowing and reaping holds true. And if we allow farming to teach us a few lessons on this matter, I think we can learn more than we might imagine.

There are five lessons from the farming principle that I find most meaningful. First, you cannot reap until you sow. It sounds simple enough, yet we forget it too soon. Often, we long for certain events to take place in life, yet we have not invested in any effort that would cause the thing we long for to materialize. You cannot harvest corn until you first plant corn, and you cannot reap spiritual blessings until you have made spiritual investments in your life. Second, you can reap only what you sow. Sowing apple seeds yields apple trees. Similarly, you cannot gain friends unless you are friendly. Conversely, if you are hateful, you will likely be hated in return. Third, you do not reap immediately after you sow. Farming is not like cooking popcorn in the microwave; you don't get what you want three minutes after you start trying. We must be patient when waiting to see the fruit of our labor. Fourth, you will reap in proportion to what you have originally sown. The Bible says, "a farmer who plants only a few seeds will get a small crop . . . But the one who plants generously will get a generous crop" (2 Cor 9:6). And finally, you will only be able to sow out of what you reap. Farming is perpetual motion. Sowing does not end with reaping, and reaping does not end with sowing. As we plant, we are able to harvest, and from what we harvest, we are again able to plant. Imagine how this principle can apply to friendship, marriage, business dealings, acts of benevolence, and a whole range of life events and relationships.

Sowing and reaping imagery is certainly not unique to Christian theology. Take, for instance, the eastern notion of karma. Found in ideologies such as Hinduism, Buddhism, and Jainism, karma suggests that life operates on the principle of cause and effect such that every deed results in a corresponding consequence. The principle, we may argue, is fairly universal. The biblical application, however, is unique in that God is seen as the source of all blessings—and it is indeed God who provides the benefits of a life well lived. We plant, God blesses, and therefore, we are able to reap the blessing. Far from being a mere law of nature, sowing and reaping is seen as a God-ordained principle that governs how we live when we choose to walk in the Spirit. Because of this, Paul is able to offer the believers in Galatia some practical advice on Christian living. In this segment of his letter, Paul deals primarily with the issue of generosity. Specifically, he gives his readers three clear admonitions.

Distribute the Weight

Living in the Spirit does not mean we no longer struggle with the works of the flesh. Even the most well-intentioned believer experiences bouts of temptation. And sometimes, the weight of sin becomes too difficult to bear without the help of others. For this reason, Paul begins this section of the letter by saying, "Dear brothers and sister, if another believer is overcome by some sin, you who are godly should gently and humbly help that person back onto the right path . . . And be careful not to fall into the same temptation yourself" (Gal 6:1). When Paul wrote his letter to the Corinthian believers, he spoke of the need to rebuke and restore a particular member of the church (1 Cor 5:3–5). Here in Galatia, however, Paul does not seem to have a particular person in mind. Instead, by saying, "if another believer is overcome by sin," Paul is presenting a hypothetical situation. It is conceivable that this situation, regardless of its hypothetical nature, is common enough that it would be likely to occur in the Galatian church, if it had not occurred already.

The failure to anticipate challenges in life leaves us vulnerable. When walking across a mine-infested field, complacency is the enemy. Just because we are able to take a few steps without being blown up is no reason to believe we will never step on the land mines in front of us. At this point, taking a leisurely stroll across such a field could prove to be fatal. Likewise, just because Christ has freed us from a life of sin does not mean the temptation to sin again no longer lurks on the horizon. In fact, it may very well be that the enemy's attempts to lure us to sin become even more pronounced after we become followers of Christ. It is very likely that in the course of living the Christian life along with other believers, one of us will fall into sin during a moment of complacency or weakness.

Paul gives us advice on how to deal with members of the church who are losing their battles against sin. It is here that the fruit of the Spirit plays a major role, because sinners helping sinners is like the blind leading the blind. How can I, as one who likewise struggles with sin, also help others in their struggle against the works of the flesh? Only with the help of the Holy Spirit! We need the Spirit of God to counteract our tendency to deal with sinners inappropriately. On the one hand, some of us tend to ignore the sins of others, not wanting to involve ourselves in their affairs. On the other hand, some of us deal with sinners so harshly that we leave little room for them to seek restitution. The Holy Spirit helps us love sinners so that we come to care enough to help them out of their condition. At the same time, he gives us the ability to deal with sinners firmly but gently. In the end, the goal of coming alongside sinners is not condemnation but restoration.

As we are led by the Spirit, we need to keep in mind four components of restoring a fallen brother or sister. First, it begins with those who are godly. Often, sinners fall so deeply into sin that they are either unable to work their way out or unwilling to change their ways. In such cases, the spiritually-minded believer has a responsibility to initiate the restoration process. Second, we must cultivate an attitude of gentleness and humility when helping others. There is a very real tendency to feel superior toward those who are weak. Remember, Greek culture had a tendency to frown on humility because it was viewed as a posture of weakness. Paul reminds us, however, that humility is a noble quality we need to keep us from being arrogant in our attempt to rescue others from the downward spiral of sinful behavior. Third, we help sinners by keeping them on the right track. In fact, the New Testament word for "restore" is a medical term that refers to the act of mending a fractured bone—straightening bones that are misaligned. Even in English, we talk about keeping people on the straight and narrow. When we help the sinner, we want him or her to return to living a life that is properly aligned with the will of Christ. Fourth, we should guard ourselves from falling into the same temptations as the fallen believer. We who are godly are just as susceptible to sin as anyone else, and it would be unwise to think we are immune from being tempted as others are. It is prudent, in fact, to examine ourselves before pointing out the weaknesses of others. As Jesus himself reminded us, "First get rid of the log in your own eye; then you will see well enough to deal with the speck in your friend's eye" (Matt 7:5).

Paul went on to say, "Share each other's burdens, and in this way obey the law of Christ" (Gal 6:2). Dealing with temptation and sin is likened to lifting burdens. The word "burden" literally means "a heavy load," a "weight," or "pressure," but figuratively it can also be understood as "demands made by authority." The Roman Empire, for instance, imposed a burdensome taxation system on its citizens, which made it difficult for some to enjoy the fruit of their own labor. Sin may be pleasurable, but it is also a demanding taskmaster. Temptation, likewise, creates an incredible pressure in the heart of anyone who struggles to live a godly life. The pressures of temptation and sin can only be addressed with the help of others. This is especially true when one is weak—and let's face it, we all experience moments of weakness. In times like these, we need others to help us carry the load. By myself, I may not be able to withstand the pressures around me, but with help from others, my ability to cope is strengthened. We can all think of a time when we had to carry a heavy load. Take, for instance, a large sofa. On our own, the task seems impossible, but once a friend comes to help, the work suddenly becomes bearable. Something good happens when we help carry one another's burdens.

When we help others, we are, in effect, obeying the law of Christ, which is the law of love. When confronted with the woman caught in adultery (John 8:1–11), the woman's accusers demanded that she be punished in accordance to the law. Without necessarily dispensing with the law, Jesus took a higher road and offered the woman forgiveness and restoration, with the admonition that she should no longer live in sin. Imagine the burden lifted from this woman's shoulders! Even though she was brought to Jesus for punishment, she was instead met by love and understanding. This woman would undoubtedly live the rest of her life remembering how gracious Jesus was and how his love brought about her restoration. We who are made godly by grace should treat others as Christ treated her. After all, Jesus reminded us, "as I have loved you, you should love each other" (John 13:34).

In case there were still those in the Galatian church who felt they were too godly to help weak sinners, Paul wrote, "If you think you are too important to help someone, you are only fooling yourself . . . You are not that important" (Gal 6:3). Arrogance can raise its ugly head when we are surrounded by people whose struggles we do not share. I have never struggled with drug addiction (unless you consider donuts a drug), so I tend to be unsympathetic toward people who can't seem to overcome their dependence on drugs. Even worse, I also tend to feel superior to them, since I have kept my life virtually drug-free. My arrogance, however, serves no good purpose either for me or for the addicted person. When my soul is tainted with pride, it keeps me from being compassionate toward those who could use my help.

Living with such vain conceit is a form of fooling ourselves, because we forget all too quickly that we too were once in need of deliverance from sin. It is only by the grace of God that we have arisen from our state of spiritual corruption. If we think we accomplished all this on our own, we are deluded beyond measure. Paul gave a similar warning to the believers in Rome when he said, "Don't think you are better than you really are . . . Be honest with your evaluation of yourselves, measuring yourselves by the faith God has given us" (Rom 12:3). Think about it: If Jesus was willing to stoop down to our level in order to save us from sin, who are we to refuse to stoop down in order to help others overcome theirs?

Clean Up Your Closet

Human behavior is fascinating. I'm especially curious as to why we tend to be most judgmental toward others in areas in which we personally struggle. A few years ago, a preacher who adamantly condemned homosexuality was himself caught in a homosexual affair. Then there's the finance guru who had to file for bankruptcy. Or how about the environmentalist who criticized those ruining the rain forests only to be called out on his million-dollar vacation cottage made of lumber from an endangered species of trees? Hypocrisy happens all the time, and although we may not be guilty of it on as large a scale as those I've mentioned, we all still struggle with the tendency to judge others before we clean up our own act.

This is not a modern phenomenon. Even in the first century, Paul was fully aware of the need to put one's own affairs in order. That is why he reminded the Galatians, "Pay careful attention to your own work, for then you will get the satisfaction of a job well done, and you won't need to compare yourself to anyone else" (Gal 6:4). Just as Socrates spoke of the folly of an unexamined life, Paul teaches us to pay attention to our lives and the work we do. After teaching the Galatians to care for those who have fallen into sin and warning them against falling into the same state, Paul reminds us it is also important to care for ourselves.

Caring for our "own work" is not limited to our career or vocation; rather, it encompasses everything we do as a matter of lifestyle. This certainly includes our jobs, but it also involves our personal responsibilities, our domestic obligations, our social responsibilities, and our ministry in the church. Paul gives two reasons as to why we need to keep our own closets clean. First, we will enjoy the satisfaction of a job well done. Rewards are great motivators, and they come in many forms. Workers are rewarded with regular paychecks, athletes are rewarded with trophies and medals, actors are rewarded with Oscars and Emmys, and outstanding employees get a special parking space for a month. There is something satisfying about being recognized for our achievements. But rewards can be a double-edged sword. When we get used to being rewarded for every accomplishment, we soon find it difficult to do anything unless we are sure to be noticed. And let's face it—not everything we do is noticed, nor is every good work publicly acknowledged. And worse, some of us might do good works only if we know a reward awaits; if no reward is imminent, we end up doing mediocre work or slacking altogether. There must surely be something more rewarding than a mere plaque or cheap trophy. There is! It is called the satisfaction of a job well done. If we are ultimately content with knowing the work we do is our very best, then we are free from the impulse to seek other people's approval. Besides, God always knows what we do, and in the end, the greatest reward comes from him.

A second reason for taking care of our personal lives is so that we will have no need to compare ourselves with others. Jealousy and envy are poisons that destroy an otherwise healthy individual. When we are constantly comparing ourselves with others, we are robbed of the joy that comes from knowing we are uniquely created by God. Our appearance, our skills and abilities, our personality, our achievements, and our passions are all part of what makes us a person unlike any other. Even the psalmist reminds us that we are God's workmanship made to be so "wonderfully complex" (Ps 139:14). Immature people always judge themselves against others, while mature people judge themselves against God's purpose and will for them. It is surprising to realize that what we long for in others is often already ours in a unique and special way.

In his famous lecture entitled "Acres of Diamonds," the American Baptist minister Russell Conwell tells the story of a Persian farmer named Ali Hafed.[1] He owned a large tract of land lush with all kinds of vegetation and grains and was therefore very wealthy, and for the most part, Ali Hafed was content. But one day, a man told him about diamonds and argued that a person could not be truly rich unless he possessed jewels. Suddenly, Hafed became restless and discontent, dreaming each night that he might possess tons and tons of diamonds. Unable to hold in his frustrations, Hafed sold his land and journeyed around the world to find this precious gem. Unfortunately, he soon became broke and depressed. Feeling defeated, Hafed eventually committed suicide. Sometime later, the man who bought Hafed's farm saw something shimmering on the ground. It was a diamond! As it turned out, the farm sat on what was soon discovered to be one of the richest diamond mines in history—the Golkonda diamond mine. Ironically, Hafed lost his life searching for something he already had. If he had learned not to compare himself with others, he would have enjoyed the blessing that was already his if he had only been willing to explore the land he already had.

Paul concluded this section on personal responsibility by saying, "For we are each responsible for our own conduct" (Gal 6:5). As a young believer, I first read this verse out of the King James Version of the Bible, which says, "For every man shall bear his own burden." This rendering was a bit confusing because it seemed to contradict Paul's previous command to bear "one another's burdens" (Gal 5:2). Why would Paul tell us to carry other people's burdens and then tell us to bear our own burden? This apparent contradiction is easily explained through an examination of Paul's original language. The word "burden" in the second verse is actually not

---

1. See Russell Herman Conwell, *Acres of Diamonds* (New York: Harper, 1915).

identical to the word "burden" in the fifth verse. In the second verse, Paul used the term *baros*, which suggests a heavy load that requires more than one person to carry. In the fifth verse, Paul used the term *phortion*, which is a light, personal pack (similar to the modern backpack) that can be easily carried by one person. In other words, while Paul encouraged us to help others carry loads that are too heavy to be carried alone, he also reminds us to take care of our own responsibilities, which others are not to carry for us. In this sense, the New Living Translation is clearer when it says, "we are each responsible for our own conduct." When our neighbor needs to run an errand, my wife and I are more than happy to help him carry the burden of babysitting his children. However, he is still personally responsible for taking care of his children as their father—that is a burden we cannot carry for him because he has to carry that pack himself.

In our modern culture, we have seen a rise in the victim mentality that tempts us to hold others responsible for what happens in our lives. Although other people may certainly be culpable for some of our problems, we need to sift through our personal affairs and identify our own responsibilities. That way, we don't make the mistake of thinking everything that goes wrong in our lives must be somebody else's fault. If we learn to keep our own closets clean, we greatly reduce the risk of being the victim of the devil's accusations and temptations. That leaves us in the best position to help others in need.

Give Your Teachers an Apple

Paul goes on to offer useful advice on how to share our resources with others. Although he does not specifically mention money, it is strongly implied that investing our money wisely is very much a part of how our resources are shared with those in need. Money is a very personal subject, and I know for a fact that when I preach on anything related to it, some in our congregation become understandably uneasy. Yet to ignore the issue is to do a great disservice to anyone who seeks to be a serious disciple of Jesus Christ. Interestingly, Jesus spoke of wealth more than any other single topic—even more than prayer and faith! Why do you suppose this is so? Could it be that money often represents the one thing in our lives that we hold so dear it can actually get in the way of our complete devotion to God? In his letter to young Timothy, Paul wrote about a companion who had deserted him for the world: "Demas has deserted me because he loved the things of this life and has gone to Thessalonica" (2 Tim 4:10). We know very little about Demas, but it is clear that he was once a faithful companion to Paul. In fact, he is called a fellow laborer of the apostle (Phil 23-24) and a fellow servant along with Luke (Col 4:12-14). Yet for some reason, Demas was so lured by the temptations of the world that he eventually abandoned Paul in favor of returning to a life of worldliness. We are not told exactly what lured him, but it is conceivable that it had something to do with wealth and pleasure.

How then do we resist our tendency to be lured by worldly wealth? Paul suggests that we must learn how to share our wealth with those in need. He begins with our relationship with our teachers. Paul said, "Those who are taught the word of God should provide for their teachers, sharing all good things with them" (Gal 6:6). In the ancient world, teachers negotiated teaching fees in a variety of ways. Some did not charge any particular amount and simply accepted what was voluntarily given to them. Others would charge a set fee for their lectures. Some even charged fees but made sure that the proceeds were shared with the students in order to augment their meager allowances while pursuing their studies.

But there was a new kind of teacher that emerged in the first century—the Christian church teacher. This person was not necessarily a professional teacher but one who was gifted in instructing believers in Christian living. As such, these teachers did not necessarily earn the typical salary afforded to credentialed instructors. But as these teachers began to give more and more of their time to the task of educating God's people, it became necessary for them to rely on the kindness of the church to provide for their needs. Paul had an interestingly balanced view on how ministers were to be supported. One the one hand, he believed it was better for a minister to work a trade rather than impose a financial burden on a church that was not prepared to provide its minister enough support. This is especially true for ministers involved in pioneering work such as planting new churches. Paul, being a missionary church planter, often worked as a tent maker (Acts 18:3) in order to support his ministry endeavors since the churches he worked with were not yet stable enough to provide for his financial needs. On the other hand, he urged churches to do their best, as they were able, to give ministers ample support for their work. Paul also explained this position to the church in Corinth when he wrote,

> Don't you realize that those who work in the temple get their meals from the offerings brought to the temple? And those who serve at the altar get a share of the sacrificial offerings. In the same way,

the Lord ordered that those who preach the good news should be supported by those who benefit from it. Yet I have never used any of these rights. (1 Cor 9:13–15)

As a young minister in the Philippines, I used to conduct Bible studies with people who lived in the slums of Manila. I always raised my own money to travel to and from the village, and I never expected the people there to give me any financial support for teaching them the Bible. One night, however, after a time of teaching and ministry, I started to walk to the bus station. As I began to board the bus, the village leader came running while hollering my name. When I looked back, he caught up to me and said, "We all took up a collection, and we want you to have this." Then he handed me a ten-peso bill. It really wasn't much—at that time it was about fifty cents in American currency—but I know it took a great deal for them to come up with that amount. I knew they needed the money more than I did, so I tried to give it back. But what he said to me changed my thinking forever. He shoved the money back in my hand, clasped it between both of his, and said, "Please Pastor Ed, don't rob us of this blessing." What an amazing response! Believe me, I've been among wealthy misers who wouldn't even think of supporting a young minister like me. The people in those slums touched me deeply that day. They displayed a depth of spiritual maturity that can only be reached by yielding to the ministry of the Word and of the Holy Spirit.

It is important to note that Paul wanted the Galatians to distinguish between false teachers and godly teachers. He told them to support those who "taught the Word of God," not the wisdom of men. Supporting such ministers should not be seen as a burdensome act, but rather as a gracious way of partnering with God's leaders in the work of the ministry.

Make Heavenly Investments

Another way we can share our resources is to make heavenly investments. Paul wrote, "Don't be misled—you cannot mock the justice of God . . . You will always harvest what you plant" (Gal 6:7). Investing in the kingdom of God is based on the principle of sowing and reaping. This principle, widely known by those in the farming industry, would have been familiar to the Galatian believers since most regions in the ancient world were deeply dependent on local agriculture. Farmers know that the seeds thrown to the ground are not wasted; rather, they are invested into the soil in order to reap a bountiful crop during the season of harvest.

Reap It Good

The scientific world introduced us to the principle that mass is conserved. In simple terms, we know that matter is never created nor destroyed in an isolated system; instead, matter simply changes from one form or another. So when we burn a piece of paper, the mass of the paper does not disappear, it simply takes on a different form. In a spiritual sense, the resources of God are neither created nor destroyed by us. We simply pass them on from one person to another, making spiritual resources investments that will sprout into other forms of blessings. By arguing that we "cannot mock the justice of God," Paul is saying that the principles of God cannot be defied. This is especially true of the principle of sowing and reaping—we will *always* reap what we sow. There is no way to skirt around this tenet.

When applied to moral behavior, the principle of sowing and reaping works this way: "Those who live only to satisfy their own sinful nature will harvest decay and death from that sinful nature . . . But those who live to please the Spirit will harvest everlasting life from the Spirit" (Gal 6:8). What a stark contrast between the works of the flesh and the fruit of the Spirit! It is essential that we realize that all our actions yield specific consequences. If we invest in worldly things, we may gain temporary satisfaction and feed our temporal pleasures, but in the end, the eternal state of our soul is at stake. If, however, we invest in what pleases the Holy Spirit, we will not only enjoy spiritual blessings we can share with others, we will also gain eternal blessing in the presence of God.

As a pastor of a local church, I cannot escape the business side of running an organization. This means making choices in how we use the funds entrusted to us by our generous supporters. We live in a world that requires us to spend money in order to minister. Like any other organization, the church needs to pay the salaries of its staff, cover utility bills, pay for goods and services, maintain facilities, and support other ministers and missionaries. All these responsibilities require money. But before we shell out a single dollar, a vital spiritual question must be asked: *What kind of investment is this in terms of the work of God's kingdom?* If we cannot answer that question properly, then we are misusing the church's money. The answer to this question is not given in terms of currency but in terms of lives touched with the gospel of Jesus Christ. We don't buy an amplification system simply to sound great but to clearly communicate the love of Christ through song and spoken Word. We don't pay for roof repairs just to have a nice looking building but to provide a safe place for people to congregate and be ministered to. We don't help missionaries for the sake of easing our conscience but to make sure the Christian gospel reaches places that have not yet heard the glorious message of eternal life through Jesus Christ. By using our resources this way, we are making heavenly investments in order to reap a bountiful spiritual harvest, all for the glory of God.

Lest we become jaded from all the appeals to help needy people in our cities and around the world, we need to keep in mind that nothing we give for the sake of Christ is ever wasted. Paul reminded the Galatians, "So let's not get tired of doing what is good . . . At just the right time we will reap a harvest of blessing if we don't give up" (Gal 6:9). Anything we do continuously and repeatedly eventually exhausts us, even if what we are doing is good. What's more, it is difficult to sustain a good thing when we don't see immediate results. Earlier we noted there is a gap between the time of sowing and the time of reaping. That waiting period can be particularly excruciating. It may seem nothing is happening, but in reality, far more is taking place than we can see or imagine. And in due time, the seeds we sow will produce a bountiful harvest that will make the wait worth it. The key is to never give up.

The enemy of good farming is impatience. When my dad was a young lad, he saw the family gardener working the soil. He asked what was going on, and the gardener explained he was planting seeds that would someday sprout up as a plant. Later that day, my grandmother saw my dad squatting in the garden, staring intently at the soil. "What are you doing?" asked my grandmother. "I'm waiting for the plant to pop out of the ground," my dad answered. When she asked when the seed was planted, he responded, "This morning." After a hearty laugh, my grandmother had to explain it would take some time before that would happen. Sure enough, in time the plant sprouted from the soil, and my dad was finally able to enjoy the moment he was waiting for.

Likewise, a farmer must wait a good amount of time between planting and harvesting, and if the farmer is patient, he will see the fruit of all that hard work. Are you tired of doing good? Does it seem like your deeds go unnoticed? Have you ever felt that your acts of kindness never really make a difference? Hang in there, and at the right time, God will reward your patience. There's no need to concern ourselves with the future because that is all in God's hands. As my dear friend once reminded me, we should not worry about the future because God is already there.

Adoniram Judson was a man who never tired of doing good. In the early 1800s, he and his wife went to Burma as missionaries. He soon discovered that the Burmese people were not initially drawn to the Christian gospel. In fact, he faced a great deal of opposition in the course of his ministry there. It would be six years before he saw anyone dedicate their life to Christ. In the first twelve years of his mission, he recorded only eighteen conversions to Christ—unimpressive by any standard. Most missionaries would have given up at this point, convincing themselves that this was not God's will for their lives. But not Judson. He remained in Burma, where he would serve for almost forty years. By the end of his ministry, Judson had translated the Bible into Burmese and left a legacy of about a hundred churches. When he first arrived in Burma, there were hardly any known Christians in the country. By the time of his death, over eight thousand believers had professed faith in Jesus Christ. Because Judson had sown abundantly, in time, he reaped a great harvest of souls for Christ. Paul was right in reminding us that we should never get tired of doing what is good.

Paul closes this section of the letter with a reminder to remain vigilant. He writes, "Therefore, whenever we have the opportunity, we should do good to everyone—especially those in the family of faith" (Gal 6:10). Opportunities abound even when we don't see any. A few years ago, I had just completed a bank deposit and began to leave. The customer in front of me was a large man in a dingy construction outfit and had arms riddled with tattoos (I must admit that I was rather intimidated). As he stepped out, he let go of the door, not knowing I was behind him. The door would have certainly slammed into my face were it not for my quick reflexes. "Oh, I'm sorry," he said, "I didn't see you." I brushed it off by saying, "Boy, if that door hit me, it would have been a bad start to my day!" He responded, "You think you'd have a bad day—I'm on my way to a chemotherapy treatment right now." My heart sank. I walked alongside him as he headed to his truck and listened as he spoke about his battle with cancer. When we got to his truck, I asked him, "Do you mind if I say a prayer for you right now?" He looked a little puzzled, but he agreed. I said a very simple and short prayer for him, asking God to be with him in this difficult time of his life. After we prayed, I looked up at him and saw tears streaming down his cheeks. He told me no one had ever done anything like that for him before. Before we parted, I gave him my card and told him to call me anytime. As I walked toward my car, he yelled from across the parking lot, "That was really, really cool . . . Thank you!" None of it was planned—at least not by me. But it was an opportunity to bless someone at a time when I could have easily been absorbed with the busy demands of my own day.

Fooling Ourselves with Fig Leaves

We don't have to be materially wealthy to be generous. We have so many other assets beyond money. We can always share our time, our presence, and even our story. Until we step out of our comfort zones and find opportunities to bless others, we will never know the joy of sharing the abundance of blessings that are already ours in Christ Jesus. Sometimes, we simply need to be the miracle someone is praying for.

The Christian life is about making eternal investments. Let's not forget the lesson of the farmer—if we sow abundantly, we will reap abundantly.

13

Just One More Thing
Galatians 6:11–18

THE 1970S WAS A great decade for TV police dramas. Shows like *Baretta*, *The Rockford Files*, *Harry O*, *Kojak*, *Adam 12*, *Mannix*, *Police Woman*, *S.W.A.T.*, and *Ironside* were just a few of my favorites. My absolute favorite, however, was *Columbo*. Peter Falk played the role of Lieutenant Columbo, a homicide detective working for the Los Angeles Police Department. Unlike the other TV cops, he dressed in a shabby raincoat, didn't drive a fancy car, smoked cigars, appeared awkwardly clueless, and hardly even carried a gun. But Columbo was a great investigator. His eye for detail was impeccable, and he had the ability to interview people without making them feel he suspected them of a crime. I especially liked his style of questioning key suspects. He would ask a few questions, thank the person for their time, and walk away as if the interview were over. But a few seconds later, he would pause, turn around, and say to the disarmed suspect, "Just one more thing . . ." Columbo would follow up with a question that would totally damage the suspect's alibi.

There is something Columboesque about the way the Apostle Paul ends his letter to the Galatians. He has pretty much said everything he needed to say. He dealt with the problem of the Judaizers, clarified the role of the law, expressed concern over how the gospel was being perverted, reinforced the doctrine of justification by faith alone, and offered practical advice on how to live as people set free by of the redemptive work of Christ and empowered by the Holy Spirit. He offered pointed reminders on the importance of taking personal responsibility. He charged each Galatian believer to take care of others without forsaking his or her own personal duties. Paul seemed confident that his words would not fall on deaf ears and trusted the Galatians would embrace his instructions wholeheartedly.

But Paul is also a realist. He understood that even the best-intentioned individuals need to be encouraged to continue doing what is right. He was aware that the false teachers would not give up so easily in trying to undermine the work of the gospel. So before bidding his readers farewell, Paul seems to be prepared to walk away. But then he pauses, and as if to turn around and say, "Just one more thing . . ." before leaving the Galatians with one more set of instructions.

Don't Be Fooled Again

Paul begins this section with an extremely interesting comment. He writes, "NOTICE WHAT LARGE LETTERS I USE AS I WRITE THESE CLOSING WORDS IN MY OWN HANDWRITING" (Gal 6:11). Paul is credited as the author of almost half the books of the New Testament. But that doesn't mean he personally penned each and every one of his letters. Instead, he often used a writing secretary, known as an *amanuensis*. Paul's amanuensis would have been responsible for jotting down Paul's words as he dictated them. His letter to the Galatians was largely composed in this manner. It would seem, however, that at this particular point in the letter, Paul took the pen from his secretary to personally write down this line.

There are several reasons why Paul would do this. First, including a personal handwritten line would help authenticate the document. The growth of the Christian church in the early centuries saw a rise in pseudographs, or forgeries of apostolic writings. If, for instance, a writer wanted the church to accept a particular teaching but was afraid his authority would be questioned, he could simply sign the document in the name of a recognized apostle to give the appearance of apostolic authority. This would be equivalent to me writing a book but ascribing its authorship to Billy Graham. In order to leave no doubt that Paul was indeed the author of the Galatian letter, he made sure his own handwriting was present in the document. A second reason for writing a line in his own hand was to emphasize the urgency of the point Paul was about to make. It's as if he was letting the Galatians know what he was about to say was of utmost importance. Thus, he did not want his secretary to "speak" for him in this matter.

It is equally interesting to note that Paul used large letters when writing this portion of the epistle. We can only guess why. One theory is that the largeness of the print was for emphasis—much like we would use bold or italicized fonts in a modern document. Others have theorized that the large letters substantiate the belief that Paul suffered from poor eyesight, causing him to write words large enough for him to read. Still others have suggested that the years of tent-making had so damaged Paul's hands that he could only writing in large strokes. No one knows for sure why Paul wrote this way. All we know is that Paul felt it was important enough for him to mark this letter with his personal stamp.

The first of Paul's final instructions was a warning against false teachers. These wolves in sheep's clothing had fooled the Galatians once already, and Paul did not want them to be fooled again. He tells them, "Those who are trying to force you to be circumcised want to look good to others . . . They don't want to be persecuted for teaching that the cross of Christ alone can save" (Gal 6:12). Describing the Judaizers as "those who are trying to force you to be circumcised" reiterates Paul's previous warning against giving in to false teachers' demands to be circumcised against their will. Again, Paul was not saying that being circumcised was a bad thing but that since it was not necessary for salvation, circumcision should be seen as purely elective for Gentile believers. Not only was it wrong for the Judaizers to force this practice on the Galatians, they also had impure motives for doing so. In this case, the Judaizers were only looking after their own best interests. They knew that failure to push for circumcision would result in criticism from the Jewish community. Also, those who did not understand its significance considered preaching salvation through the cross of Christ foolish. So as it turned out, the Judaizers' insistence on circumcising the Galatians was not necessarily for the good of the church but was instead intended to protect their own reputation in the community. These false teachers were not to be trusted primarily because they were not truly sincere.

Sincerity is quickly becoming a rare commodity. So much of what people do today is tainted with ulterior motives. I remember once when my eldest son was only a few months old and Ana and I were shopping at the local grocery store with little Jonathan neatly tucked in his baby carrier atop the shopping cart. A woman walked up to us and said, "Wow, what a beautiful baby!" After exchanging pleasantries, she handed us her business card and said, "If you are in the market to buy a house, be sure to give me a call." Are you kidding me? She wasn't really interested in how adorable my baby was—she just wanted to make a sale. Her apparent lack of sincerity turned us off.

Unfortunately, these things happen all too often. But it is somehow worse when sincerity comes from the mouths of religious teachers. You would expect such people to be pure in their motives. But this was not the case in the Galatian church. Nor is it necessarily the case with some churches today. We've heard too many stories of preachers and teachers using the ministry for personal gain—but not so with Paul. Although he was sometimes viewed as harsh, Paul was certainly not insincere. Even at the risk of being criticized or misunderstood, Paul preached the gospel out of God's love. He showed us that the only true motivation for undertaking ministry is love for God, because without it we cannot love others as we should.

Paul continued to expose the Judaizers' insincerity when he wrote, "And even those who advocate circumcision don't keep the whole law themselves . . . They only want you to be circumcised so that they can boast about it and claim you as their disciples" (Gal 6:13). Ministry can often become a game of who can attract the most followers. If you put a group of pastors together in a room, the conversation will inevitably lead to comparing how many parishioners each one has. The unmentioned rule of the game is that the pastor with the most members wins. This game is difficult to play, especially when your church is young or struggling. During the early years of our church planting efforts, I was often asked, "How many members do you have now?" I would grasp at numbers, counting all the active members, then including every living being that might have been in our meeting room the past Sunday, wanting to add in insects, rodents, and anything else with the breath of life in it. My motive was to make things look better than they really were.

Paul, on the other hand, was not interested in playing this game. In fact, he accused the false teachers of simply using the Galatians as mere pawns in their games. They did not care for the people as shepherds care for their sheep. Instead, they saw people simply as a means to obtain bragging rights. Ironically, the false teachers were not even keen on obeying the very laws they imposed on the members of the church as further evidence of their lack of sincerity.

Paul said all this to warn the people against being fooled by hypocrites—a warning we would be wise to heed even today. Not long ago, a man sought to build a perfect society. He proudly displayed his worn-out Bible to demonstrate his religiosity, he told stories of God's blessings, professed faith in the Christian message, and insisted all he wanted to do was the will of God. Yes, Adolf Hitler might fool more than a few unsuspecting followers. The results of his hypocritical leadership were certainly devastating. Germans today reject the cause of this madman and have resolved never again to be fooled by such a character. In the same way, Paul did his best to convince the Galatians (and believers today) not to fall for the lies of those who seek to lead without sincerity and are only pursuing personal gain in the name of religion.

Keep the Main Thing the Main Thing

Paul took every measure to distance himself from the false teachers in Galatia. As he ends his letter, he makes one final effort. He writes, "As for me, may I never boast about anything except the cross of our Lord Jesus Christ... Because of that cross, my interest in the world has been crucified, and the world's interest in me has also died" (Gal 6:14). After accusing the Judaizers of being self-centered hypocrites who sought only to boast about themselves, Paul asserts that any boasting from him can only be about his Master, Jesus Christ. Specifically, he boasts about the cross of Christ. This is an interesting contrast to the false teachers' boasting, especially considering that both circumcision and crucifixion were sometimes thought to be forms of bodily mutilation. So while the "mutilation" of the foreskin has no merit with regards to salvation, the "mutilation" of the body of Christ on the cross not only has merit, it is also the only means of atonement for our sins.

The doctrine of atonement is central to the work of Jesus Christ on the cross. In the Bible, the word "atone" carries ideas of covering and reconciliation. In essence, the death of Christ covered and washed away our sins, which made it possible for us to be reconciled with God. There are four dimensions to atonement that make it meaningful for each believer. The first is *necessity*. The death of Christ was necessary because there was no other way for us to be saved. Neither works of righteousness nor personal attempts at piety are sufficient to attain a right relationship with God. Second is *substitution*. Because we are not able to save ourselves, Jesus died on the cross in our place. His work is completed on our behalf. The third is *propitiation*. A word we hardly use in modern English, "propitiation" refers to the act of appeasement. In this case, the death of Christ fully appeased the demands of the law and of the holiness of God. Finally, there is *imputation*, which means to credit one's assets to another person's account. The death of Christ was the exact payment needed for the penalty of sin. But since Jesus had no sin to atone for, the payment is credited to the account of those who put their faith in him. Atonement is at once one of the most significant and most beautiful doctrines of the Christian faith.

Yet atonement is also a divisive doctrine because those who seek to be saved by works do not accept its premise. But Paul does not allow himself to be detracted by his critics. Instead, he freely gives up approval from others by crucifying his personal interest upon the cross of Christ. Consequently, the world has also lost interest in Paul. Yet all is well for Paul because he has chosen to live only for the approval of God.

In a final effort to keep the Galatians focused on what mattered most, Paul wrote, "It doesn't matter whether we have been circumcised or not . . . What counts is whether we have been transformed into a new creation" (Gal 6:15). The best way to address the issue of circumcision was to make it a non-issue. Essentially, Paul was saying it was fine to be circumcised but that it was also fine to remain uncircumcised. Circumcision, after all, is not what is important when it comes to the matter of righteousness. This is such an important lesson for modern believers. Too often, we make a big deal over things that have no eternal importance.

Toward the middle of the twentieth century, communism was gaining ground in Eastern Europe. During that time, some churches were arguing over what color robes priests should wear during each week of the Christmas season. Can you imagine that? While the geopolitical landscape was being transformed, religious people were arguing over fabric color! Talk about being out of touch. Yet we are in danger of making the same mistake in our own generation in a time when nations are at war, children are being orphaned, people are dying of starvation, and homes are being torn apart. How can we possibly focus on the trivial when so many important matters demand our attention? What is keeping us from paying heed to what is truly important?

Paul said we should be most concerned about our transformation as new creations in Christ Jesus. Elsewhere he said,

> . . . anyone who belongs to Christ has become a new person. The old life is gone; a new life has begun! And all of this is a gift from God, who brought us back to himself through Christ. And God has given us this task of reconciling people to him. For God was in Christ, reconciling the world to himself, no longer counting people's sins against them. And he gave us this wonderful message of reconciliation. (2 Cor 5:17–19)

Metamorphosis from sinner to saint is not intended to be enjoyed privately. Yes, it is true that we greatly benefit from no longer pursuing the works of the flesh, but it is also important that others benefit as well. As transformed beings, we are in a position to help others realize the gift of salvation through Jesus Christ. Paul specifically uses the term "reconciliation," which means "to exchange." Because of Christ, we are each able to exchange our old life for a new one—trading alienation from God for friendship with God. We who have experienced this great exchange are now called to be agents of reconciliation for the sake of others. Do you know anyone who has yet to be reconciled back to God? You need to understand the blessing of salvation that is given to you compels you to share this gift with such people. When we make it our life mission to love God and others through the ministry of reconciliation, we find that we actually have no time to waste on things that ultimately don't matter.

There is something special about people using their God-given freedom to bring the message of the gospel to those still enslaved by ignorance or religiosity. Paul expresses this blessing upon such people when he writes, "May God's peace and mercy be upon all who live by this principle; they are the new people of God" (Gal 6:16). The pronouncement of "peace and mercy" was a common blessing in Judaism. It was to wish upon others a life of wholeness and bliss, which is only possible through the favor of God. We are at peace when the presence of God accompanies us, even when we go through turbulent times. We are recipients of God's mercy only because of his love and kindness. With no regard as to whether or not we deserve it, God freely grants forgiveness to those who are willing to receive it, on account of what Jesus Christ has done for us at the cross. This dual blessing of peace and mercy is conditioned only upon faith, not the law. As such, those of us who are unable to satisfy the demands of the law are nevertheless able to reap the blessings of God, simply because he is good.

Christians are called to "live by this principle." This means that the step of faith must be followed by the walk of faith. We do not simply rely on the blessings of the past for the rest of our lives. Instead, we continue to abide by the principles of spiritual living as we are empowered by God's Spirit to do so. In my work as a pastor, I have conducted my fair share of weddings. I worry sometimes that couples put far more effort into their wedding day than into their marriage itself. The wedding tends to be a sky-is-the-limit event—the best venue, the best food and drinks, the best music, the best flowers, the best clothes, and the company of best friends. But when the wedding is over, the term "best" fades from the scene. As some point, it almost seems as if husband and wife are merely putting up with each other. What goes wrong? I believe it is a failure to sustain the commitment of the early stages of the relationship. It is not only important to start well, it is equally important to live well. This principle is true in marriage, and it is also true in our life with Christ.

As a result of continuing our life of faith, you and I not only become new individuals, together we also become a new people. The Judaizers took great pride in being the people of God based on the Abrahamic covenant, but Paul declared that all believers today are the new people of God through the new covenant with Christ Jesus our Lord.

Focus on What Is Important

Paul makes one final request as he ends his letter to the Galatians. He asks, "From now on, don't let anyone trouble me with these things . . . For I bear on my body the scars that show I belong to Jesus" (Gal 6:17). At first glance, it might seem as if Paul was a jaded old man who did not wish to be bothered by life's frivolities. But this is not the case at all; otherwise, he would not have bothered to write an important letter addressing the different issues surrounding church life in the city of Galatia. Paul is not annoyed by people who seek his help in spiritual matters. However, once a matter has been resolved (as Paul certainly felt was the case with the Galatian controversy), there would no longer be any need to revisit, and consequently reargue, the issue.

Paul dealt with heresies at his own peril. He reminded his readers that his body bore the scars of his many years of fighting as a soldier of the gospel. At times, his scars were physical. In his letter to the Corinthians, Paul described some of the trials he faced in ministry, saying, "We patiently endure troubles and hardships and calamities of every kind . . . We have been beaten, been put in prison, faced angry mobs, worked to exhaustion, endured sleepless nights, and gone without food" (2 Cor 6:4–5). Other times, Paul's wounds were emotional. He was abandoned by his associates and betrayed by people he trusted. It's hard to decide which kind of suffering is worse: physical or emotional. In Paul's case, there was no choice to be made—he suffered both. Yet Paul gladly endured such suffering if it meant bringing clarity to others. He was indeed a man who no longer lived for himself but rather for the sake of his Master, Jesus Christ. In the ancient world, some pagans used tattoos as a form of branding. Paul had no tattoos, but he had scars to show others he belonged to Christ.

We must understand that willingness to suffer for Christ is not the same as desiring to suffer for Christ. We certainly do not wish pain upon ourselves. No one in their right mind clamors for pain. And so Paul asks the Galatians to refrain from giving him an unnecessary burden to bear. Instead, readers are encouraged to live in accordance to the truth that has been revealed to them. We are no longer slaves to the law, for we are set free by God's Spirit; therefore, let us live as free people.

When we live for the cause of the gospel, we live for something tremendously meaningful. What can we live for that is greater than the very thing Jesus died for? When our lives revolve around distractions that have no eternal value, we risk living wasted lives we are certain to regret. I want to wake up each day and know I will do something that matters. If we learn anything from Paul's letter to the Galatians, it is that the good news of salvation through Jesus Christ's redemptive work on the cross is the most crucial information that a lost and dying world needs to know. To those who heed its call, the results are both glorious and everlasting.

Finally, Paul ends his letter with these gracious words: "Dear brothers and sisters, may the grace of our Lord Jesus Christ be with your spirit. Amen" (Gal 6:18). What started as Paul's angriest letter ends in a tone of endearment. The Galatians may have brought him some frustration, but they were still members of his spiritual family. They were his brothers and sisters, and nothing was going to change that. And so Paul pronounced on them the blessing of God's grace. We are not saved by the law but by God's merciful favor. And since it is by this grace that we are saved, it only makes sense that we continue to live in the amazing grace of our Lord and Savior Jesus Christ.

Epilogue

DURING THE AMERICAN CIVIL War, a young woman found herself engaged to a career officer. She was not set on marrying him, but the pressure from both his family and hers made resistance futile. In time, she and the officer were married.

The day after the wedding, the man gave his new bride a piece of paper. It contained a list of everything he expected her to do for him now that she was his lawfully wedded wife. The list included a number of chores such as preparing breakfast each morning, keeping his uniforms neat and pressed, making sure dinner was on the table when he came home at the end of each day, and maintaining the general upkeep of the home. As a compliant wife, she obliged, following his every demand to the letter. Each day she did what she was asked, and she hated every moment of it. The burden of her husband's demands was more than she had bargained for. Her husband showed little appreciation for all she did, and with every passing year she grew more and more unhappy.

One day, the unhappy wife got word that her husband had been killed in battle. She was saddened by the news, and yet at the same time she was relieved to be released from such a burdensome marriage.

A few years later, she entertained a young suitor who won her heart with his wit, charm, simplicity, and love. They were soon married and lived a very happy life together. Year after year, she found herself falling more and more in love with her husband.

On a beautiful spring day, this happy wife decided to clean out the attic. There she found an old dresser that belonged to her first husband. She opened the drawers and found something she had completely forgotten about—the list of all his unrealistic demands. As she read the list line by line, she thought to herself, "How interesting. I am doing all of these chores for my current husband, yet this time I thoroughly enjoy it!"

Epilogue

How could it be that this woman did chores for one husband and hated every moment of it, yet did the exact same chores for her current husband and found such pleasure in her tasks? The answer is simple—with her new husband, she had a genuinely loving relationship. As result, she had no need to pretend she had a fulfilling marriage.

How about you? Are you still married to the law, or are you now in a loving relationship with Christ the Savior? Once you put your faith in Jesus, it might surprise you to realize that you are actually living the kind of life the law previously demanded. Yet this time, you do it with a cheerful spirit and a grateful heart. Now, you are clothed in the righteousness of Christ instead of struggling to cover yourself with the feeble garment of religiosity—no longer fooling yourself with fig leaves.

www.ingramcontent.com/pod-product-compliance
Lightning Source LLC
Chambersburg PA
CBHW062003180426
43198CB00036B/2162